101 403 290 3

D1422084

SHEFFIELD HALLAM UNIVERSITY
LEARNING CENTRE
WITHDRAWN FROM STOCK

Essential School Leadership

Developing Vision and Purpose in Management

Gary Holmes

London • Philadelphia

The Management and Leadership in Education Series

Series Editor: Howard Green

Competences for School Managers Derek Esp
Educational Values for School Leadership Sylvia West
Essential School Leadership Gary Holmes

To Bridget and Henry, for support and inspiration

First published in 1993

Kogan Page Limited
120 Pentonville Road
London N1 9JN

British Library Cataloguing in Publication Data

A CIP record for this book is available from the British Library.

ISBN 0 7494 0985 1

Typeset by Saxon Graphics Ltd, Derby
Printed and bound in Great Britain by Biddles Ltd, Guildford and King's Lynn

Contents

Acknowledgements

I would like to thank the many school leaders in the UK and in North America whose testimony, experience and self-disclosure have furnished much of the background against which this book was written. I am grateful to them for sharing problems as well as successes, aspirations as well as failures. In this vein, I must also acknowledge the learning experiences furnished by fellow governors at Peers School and Temple Cowley Middle School.

My thanks are also due to my colleagues at OxCEM and in the School of Education at Oxford Brookes. In particular, Marian, Michael, John and John have done much to create a climate in which many things have become possible. I also wish to acknowledge a personal debt of scholarship to Ron Best whose friendship and encouragement have sustained me for more than a decade.

Series Editor's Foreword

The government's educational reforms have created an unprecedented rate of change in schools. They have also raised fundamental questions about the purpose of education and the nature of school management and leadership. Similar changes are occurring in other educational systems throughout the world.

In this context, there is an urgent need for all of us with an interest in education to step back and reflect on recent educational reforms, to reaffirm old truths and successful practice where appropriate, to sift out and implement the best of the new ideas, modifying or abandoning those which are a distraction from the central purpose of schools: to ensure that an education of high quality is a guaranteed opportunity for *all* our children and young people.

This series has been planned to satisfy the growing need for short, readable books designed for busy people and with a focus on single issues at the cutting edge of school management and leadership.

The books are written by reflective practitioners who are either working in schools or close to the chalk-face. The authors include heads, advisers, inspectors, education officers, trainers and governors who are trying to make sense of the recent reforms and who share a desire to make their own contribution to an improving education service in the UK. The series draws on the best of current thinking and practice. It celebrates the ideals, skills and experience of professionals in education who want to see further improvements in our schools.

Gary Holmes has wide experience of education in the UK and in North America as a teacher, team leader in schools, governor, lecturer and trainer. He is currently Director of the Oxford Centre for Education Management based at Oxford Brookes University. Most of his time is spent working with headteachers, deputies and team leaders in schools and with governors.

In the past, schools could survive, even prosper, with a very low-key approach to the tasks of leadership. Times have changed. The tasks of leadership are now much more complex and demanding and schools which do not address them with sufficient thought and commitment may fail. What characterizes successful school leadership is not one particular style or method but a consistent commitment to a few very important principles and practices.

The uniqueness of this book is that the author explores the principles and then illustrates their application with many practical examples, not ducking the critical problems and dilemmas that face school leaders. He discusses the vital task of building vision and a sense of purpose in schools; ways in which the link between leadership and the quality of learning can develop beyond the rhetoric and the task of managing people in schools or building the team. Case studies of critical dilemmas for leaders include a school 'on the way down', a teacher facing problems several years in to a generally successful career, setting priorities for the budget and dealing with 'difficult' people. Throughout the case studies, the approach is balanced, sensitive and yet direct. Finally the author examines the important issue of leadership and accountability and proposes a set of priorities as school leaders, working alongside governors, evaluate the effectiveness of their schools.

As the title implies, this book is *essential* reading for all those who have an interest in effective school leadership.

Howard Green
Eggbuckland
August 1993

Introduction

Who is this book for?

This book is written for teachers who are in senior leadership positions in schools and teachers who wish to be in those positions during their careers in education. The term 'school leader' is used throughout the book to denote this audience. For practical purposes, the term school leader usually means headteacher in most of the examples, case studies and commentaries used. However, if you are preparing yourself for a future leadership role, perhaps as a headteacher, you have as much to gain from this book as a headteacher already in post. The term school leader, in this book, therefore, means *you*.

What should you expect from this book?

As a school leader now or in the future, you have a lot of helpful literature and good advice to choose from as you try to make sense of your job and develop your own brand of successful school leadership. In this book I have tried to simplify some of those complex and often conflicting messages into the five essential components of leadership covered under the five chapter headings. The chapters are arranged in a deliberate order of priority which begins with the key component of building vision and purpose in the school. This theme of vision and purpose resurfaces throughout the book. The second chapter challenges you to put children's learning at the heart of your vision for the school and of your practice as a leader. Chapter 3 deals with both the philosophical and practical challenges of managing people as a leader. In particular it explains the impact of the 'professional ethic' in schools and relates that to building a healthy climate for educational change. Chapter 4 takes you through a range of typical dilemmas which school leaders face and in each case it invites you to be clear about what is important in the dilemma and how that relates to your leadership role in practice. The final chapter contains both discussion and advice about your accountabilities as a school leader. It presents accountability as a positive force rather than as a necessary evil.

How do these themes relate to your needs as a leader?

If you followed all the advice from the available literature on school leadership you would become a very confused and ineffective leader. While this book contains much direct advice – and indeed some prescriptions – it still leaves you a range of options in developing your own approach to the essential themes covered. Thus, the five chapters contain a small number of hard messages around which your own preferences can develop at a level of detail. The hard message from Chapter 1, for example, is that vision and purpose are not optional for the leader. Without them, your school will drift and conflict will be inevitable. The good news is that once you are committed to building a powerful vision and purpose for your school, not only do you have choices in how you do it but in doing it you also make many of the other tasks of leadership easier and more enjoyable.

Making sense of leadership

School leadership is not some new or intrusive concern. It is what it always has been: the application of reason, logic, values and political will to the achievement of educational objectives via the deployment of available resources.

To the extent that the environment in which schools operate is now infinitely more complex than it was when we were at school, then the challenge of school leadership is commensurately more demanding. Not so long ago, a school could survive – and indeed prosper – with a minimalist approach to the tasks of leadership. Modern schools which do not address those tasks with sufficient energy and commitment may fail and close.

Successful school leadership embraces a wide range of cultures and practices from the relatively autocratic to the relatively democratic, from the relatively bureaucratized to the relatively *ad hoc*. What characterizes successful school leadership is not one particular style or method but a consistent commitment to a few, very important principles. Your approach to these principles might be assessed by your response to these questions:

1. What is your business? Is your basic mission as a school frequently discussed? Widely understood? Simply and clearly expressed? Shared with all your clients?
2. Who are your clients? Schools do not exist to employ teachers. Who are you working for and to whom do you feel accountable?
3. How do you make plans and take decisions? Are your methods fit-for-purpose? How do you know that you are taking the right decisions in the right way?
4. How well are you doing as a school? How would you know?
5. How do you treat people?

These principles might be summarized as:

purposes
audiences
processes
quality and
culture.

They are not the only way of viewing the notion of school leadership, but they are a good starting point.

I originally wrote the short passage above as part of the editorial content of our OxCEM newsletter. The words were intended to convey something 'essential' about school leadership which transcended any short-term political change or passing fashion. Some time later, I was discussing with a colleague what it was that leaders do which makes a real difference to the quality of education. We both agreed how vital a sense of vision and mission were while conceding at the same time how elusive such terms were. One person's vision is another's hack ideology. We then invented a fantasy scenario in which a national figure (say, a minister with some responsibility for education) wanted to make a real difference in one important policy area; we chose adult literacy. Having chewed over all the possible things that minister might do, including spending taxpayers' money on special programmes, we finally agreed that the most powerful action would be if that minister went to the media and said something like:

> No civilized society should tolerate the levels of adult illiteracy we now tolerate. It is both a matter of pride and of economic necessity that we do something about it now. I personally will undertake to adopt three adult illiterates and to do my utmost to raise them to a threshold of acceptable literacy over the next year. I call on every educational leader in the country, starting with the vice-chancellors of all our universities, to do the same.

Remember that this was a fantasy before you think of all the practical implications of the scenario! Reflecting subsequently on the fantasy, however, it clarified for me part of the relationship between vision, leadership and action. If the purpose was unquestionably 'right', it transcended ideology: if the action was positive it invited emulation and if the language was sincere it created an energy which could overcome practical obstacles. My colleague and I both agreed that we *would* follow such a lead and then immediately felt guilty about why we weren't doing it anyway!

Leaders do things

The emphasis on vision, action and energy in modern leadership thinking has been enormously influential. Peters, Kanter and others have a tremendous amount to say to school leaders. They have taught us not to fear the language of vision and mission but to bring it alive in the act of leadership. Through all the modern research and writing on leadership we see time and again how an inspiring sense of purpose can change organizations, release discretionary effort and, baldly, make things happen. Modern school leadership is exercised against a background of uncertainty and conflict about core purposes. This surely means that vision is more and not less important than in a period of relative stasis.

Leaders have skills

It is now conventional to see the composite of leadership as comprising a range of skills and competences, as well as the traditional attributes. These are sometimes described in action terms (plan, organize, delegate) and sometimes in more reflective terms (judgement, sensitivity). There are interesting movements in the recruitment and selection of school leaders reflecting the competency focus as well as even more sophisticated models based on wider private sector experience. Teachers who apply for leadership posts, particularly headteacher posts, can expect employers to look more and more closely at these skills and competences as well as at the more traditional criteria for headship. Those who select school leaders, however, will continue to be closely interested in what kind of person you are, as well as what you can do. There are dangers in using lists of skills and attributes as tools of development for potential leaders. The danger for appointing panels is that they may miss important personal dimensions of candidates. The danger for aspiring leaders is that without some objective examination of their performance, their subjectivity when considering such lists could give a very misleading picture. Who in their hearts, for example, is able to say with any certainty that they are more than averagely tactful and sensitive in their professional dealings? The good work of the National Educational Assessment Centre (NEAC) has brought some welcome objectivity into the leadership competencies arena, but there is a long way to go. Meanwhile, the lists proliferate!

Leaders have clients and audiences

It is easy to forget how remote school leaders were barely a generation ago. Parents approached schools with trepidation and felt privileged to be granted a ten minute audience over and above their seven minute entitlement at open evening. Accountability as we now perceive it was barely understood and indeed the word only came into common educational parlance with a rash of publications following Jim Callaghan's Ruskin speech on accountability in 1975. The notion of parents – or pupils – as clients or customers is even more recent. Virtually every reader of this book will have been at school when their parents saw themselves as users or recipients of a provider-led public service. Yet the modern school leader has no option but to view parents at least as customers and clients. Clients want access, accountability and a voice at court. The school's wider audience of community, employers and prospective clients expect a regular 'turn' on stage. Media coverage has now become a vital plank in the image-building of most schools.

What about the school leader in all this? We expect him or her to have a persuasive public persona, to be adroit with the media, to be knowledgeable about finance and resource management, to be successful in attracting local sponsorship and to be endlessly available to serve any of those purposes. All this on top of being the leading educationalist in the school, a skilful manager of people and decisive decision-taker. There is a point to this reminder of how much has changed so quickly and it is this: the demands made on 'average' school leaders have substantially 'upped the ante' for those leaders, compared with very recent times. In other words, we are making far greater demands of them. Literature, advice and prescription about school leadership which additionally appear to portray an unattainably complex and daunting model of the successful leader can make this worse. It can deter those who are prudently modest about their own leadership potential yet who may nevertheless make successful leaders.

Keeping leadership attainable

We cannot afford to dissuade those who will make competent school leaders from putting themselves forward. Too much emphasis on stress, strain, complexity, change, rarefied skills and insuperable dilemmas risks precisely that. Hence this book. I hope that what it does do is to arrange some of the leadership agenda in a way which is accessible and 'biteable'. I am conscious that in presenting an optimistic and accessible survey of leadership challenges, there is still a preponderance of the 'negative'. Case studies and practical examples of good practice, unfortunately, seem to make for less insight than bad practice or problems to be solved. The best of school leaders are of course very positive people. They make light of problems in public, even when weighed down by them. They constantly seek reasons to praise, to thank and to reinforce. They interpret the world in an essentially optimistic manner and they show a constant commitment to what the school is there for.

My optimism for you, the reader, is that you will see this book as making school leadership both more understandable and more attainable. Above all, I hope that it will remind you of what is important to you as a school leader and inspire you to make a real difference to the quality of education in your school.

Chapter 1

Building Vision and Purpose in the School

Vision and successful school leadership

If you wish to be a successful school leader then sooner or later you will have to come to terms with the notion of 'vision'. All successful schools are built around a clear sense of vision and purpose. All successful school leaders have a firm grasp of educational vision and purpose and can relate that vision to the regular tasks and challenges of school leadership. In this chapter, we will approach vision from a number of angles. We will try to make sense of current perspectives on vision, mission and values in school leadership. We will see where vision comes from and which practical strategies can bring it alive. We will see how school leaders can approach the problem of competing or conflicting values and vision. We will also look for a relationship between educational vision and the practical challenges of school leadership. Most of all, we will see how vital educational vision is to building successful schools.

What is vision?

We look for a sense of vision in all aspects of public life. We expect our national leaders to develop a vision for everything that society values. We hope that the police, health services and other public bodies have a clear vision of how their efforts will contribute to our welfare and well-being. Everyone who cares about the success of schools expects those schools to embody a sense of vision and purpose and of hope for a better future. This is why any attempt to consider what is important and essential about school leadership needs to start with this difficult but vital notion of vision.

For the school leader, vision is, at its simplest, the mental image of the kind of school you are trying to build for the future. That vision includes the aspirations you have for the present and future pupils in the school, the quality of teaching and learning which you think is attainable and the values which should influence everything which happens in the school. None of this is easy. Other partners in the school's community may have competing visions. Equally, your vision of the school and its future needs to be graspable by those who will carry it out alongside you. As we will see in this chapter, vague aspirations do not constitute a vision for a school. Do not be deterred by the difficulties and problems of building vision and purpose in the school. Vision need not be mystical or mysterious. If it is to work it will be expressed in quite simple terms. It will be a picture of a better future but not of an unrealistic future. It will be a reference point by which parents, teachers, pupils and others make sense of change and face challenges. At its best, a school's vision gives everyone connected with the school a reason for wanting to do things well and for feeling real pride in what the school is achieving.

Vision is difficult!

People who have an interest in successful schools, and that includes politicians, parents, pupils, teachers and the public at large, would all agree, however, that the notion of success or of effectiveness as applied to schools is difficult to define. Different people see different factors as contributing differently to that success or effectiveness. If you are 'inside' the educational debate, as a parent or teacher, you tend to see questions of resourcing or finance as vital. Politicians tend to look for effective leadership and a relevant curriculum as well as firm outcomes. All parties look for effective teaching when they consider the notion of successful schools. Educational literature in recent years has abounded with attempts to define success or effectiveness in schooling. Much research has been aimed at sifting out the elements of success and effectiveness. Unfortunately, such attempts inevitably return to those few important notions which are easy to state but difficult to analyse. Vision is one of those notions. School leaders who look for inspiration and practical guidance from the literature tend to find that they should have vision – and values – and many other attributes, competences and traits besides. Unfortunately, unlike more conventional aspects of school leadership, such as planning, decision-making, evaluating performance and the like, vision is a daunting concept. Very few school leaders admit to being visionaries and many feel uncomfortable with the whole notion of vision. To many, the word smacks of ideology or even of fanaticism. Let us therefore try to get to grips with this elusive concept.

The 'vision thing'

When George Bush was having difficulties in his re-election campaign of 1992 he told the media that he felt he needed to get hold of the 'vision thing'. This admission was immediately seized upon as a weakness and as a source of unfavourable comparisons between Bush and his opponent Bill Clinton. Curiously enough, although vision is a difficult and ambiguous concept in leadership, everyone who followed that presidential campaign knew *exactly* what Bush meant by his comment and had a clear sense of why it was important and why Clinton was outscoring Bush on 'vision'. No one needed subtitles. Perhaps it is easier for a politician to create a sense of vision about the future than it is for a school leader. It is certainly very obvious to voters when that sense of vision is absent or unsatisfactory.

Vision and schooling

The modern literature of leadership and management in schools focuses extensively on the notions of vision and mission. This emphasis parallels the received wisdom about success and effectiveness in other kinds of organizations. Key phrases which crop up repeatedly include 'core mission', 'leadership vision' and 'effective culture and climate'. This constellation of words and phrases revolving around vision and mission is so seriously over-used in the literature of management and leadership in the 1990s that some of the terms are rapidly losing meaning.

In relating these notions to the real tasks of leadership, school leaders have been led by the pressures of educational reform into new territory. For example, in terms of marketing their schools in the modern competitive climate, school leaders are obliged to make statements about mission and vision whether or not they have seriously thought through the implications of such statements. The logic of marketing is of course that you are clear about *what* you are marketing. If the product is an elusive or difficult to define service like education then the product can be encapsulated in a 'mission statement'. School leaders are now on the whole comfortable with mission statements; they are usually similar to the more traditional school handbook item, 'Aims of the School'. Some are short and snappy, ('Building tomorrow's citizens today') and some are more measured. Some sample statements are examined later in this chapter. Let us be clear that a school's vision does not reside in simple slogans or statements of aims, however clever or succinct. As we will see, the brief summary statement of mission is only an expression of a more profound sense of purpose in a school. If that more profound purpose is missing, the mission statement has no meaning.

Vision and school accountability

School leaders are also sensitized by the debates about accountability in education to think hard about school vision and mission. In most western societies educational systems are now asked for much more concrete indicators of school success than was the case 20 years ago. The nature of the national and international debate about the purpose of education has never been more vigorous or challenging, wherever you stand in that debate. At the heart of these debates about educational reform there are always questions of vision and mission:

What kind of young people are we trying to mould in our schools? What vision of learning and development should schools promote in order to fit young people for the needs of a changing society?

Yet despite all this, there is still an unease about value-driven visionary statements at the heart of school life. There is still a degree of anxiety about devoting valuable corporate time and effort in schools into seemingly intangible areas such as mission and purposes. Experienced school leaders are very wary, for example, of seeming to take on board political views about the future of schooling and selling them as their own school's vision.

Making sense of vision

The regular day-to-day tasks of school leadership are carried out, as in other organizations, in largely pragmatic fashion. Teachers do not refer instinctively to mission statements or to statements of educational objectives when making routine decisions. When schools in some sense 'fail', the causes of failure are usually described in practical or pragmatic terms. Typical reasons advanced for the failure of schools would include:

- declining numbers,
- insufficient resources
- local political factors
- underperforming staff
- failures of leadership
- inadequate planning
- inadequate curricula

Very occasionally, lack of vision or sense of purpose is suggested as a cause of school failure. In a few celebrated instances the 'wrong' vision is cited. The troubles at William Tyndale junior school in the 1970s, for example, were a cause for much public concern and have been frequently cited as an example of the failure of 'progressive' primary school teaching methods. At the heart of that school's problems undoubtedly lay a clash of vision and values. The school's leaders and many of the teachers had a vision of the curriculum and its delivery which, eventually, proved unacceptable to the authorities.

Conversely, where the success of a school is being celebrated the causes of that success are usually described in conventional terms, including:

- strong leadership
- high-performing teachers
- well planned curricula
- buoyant rolls
- supportive parents and community
- adequate resources

Yet what is it ultimately which drives a successful school? Survival is a strong driving force as is fear of failure. However, no combination of the success factors listed above will guarantee success for a school if the sense of vision and purpose is lacking. Equally, even where many unfavourable factors are working against a school (declining numbers, poor resources, a hostile political climate), a clear vision and purpose can transcend those difficulties and move a school forward. Local education authority officers and local and national schools inspectors make interesting witnesses in this respect. Over time they see many examples of success and failure in school leadership and they are often privy to information, decisions and negotiations which are not publicly available. Informally, they will happily point to examples of schools which are 'turned around' or 'transformed', often in fairly short time periods. In your own area and in your own experience you will similarly be aware of schools which have undergone quite radical changes of fortune. In tracking down the 'true' causes of these transformations, you will hear a variety of evidence, much of it concerning the quality of leadership and the spirit or culture of the school in question. Where successful leadership does succeed in transforming a school, it does not simply mean more decisions, or even better decisions. It does not mean harsher (or less harsh) person-management. Nor does it imply a particular leadership approach. Where leadership transforms a school, it does it firstly and most importantly by showing a clear way forward to a desirable future state. Without that clear vision, no transformation can occur. Indeed, without that vision even a stable, surviving school risks much. The importance of a clear vision for your school cannot be overstated. We can reinforce that by checking against our own experience of organizational life.

Our experience of vision and leadership

Teachers who have spent their careers in a number of schools always have interesting insights into what distinguishes one school from another. Supply teachers who work, often, in literally dozens of schools in the course of a year have very sharp perceptions about these differences. When you strip away the ephemeral issues such as location, the eccentricities of individual staff, the 'clubability' of colleagues or the quality of the heating system what you are left with in favourable descriptions of school is a fascinating core of factors variously termed ethos, climate, feel, etc. Many would describe this as the underlying culture of the school. It is clearly linked with the quality of leadership in the school. Above all, this core of positive feeling about schools is about being part of an organization with a sense of purpose. Not only that, but a sense of purpose with which you identify closely and that you feel to be in some sense right. By contrast, teachers with unhappy memories of former schools point to a range of contributing factors such as ineffective leadership, poor morale, inadequate resources, etc. Again, if you reduce these factors to a distilled core, what you find is that sense of purpose, or of going somewhere – but this time conspicuous by its absence.

This linking of the notion of effective organization with the presence (or absence) of vision is not unique to schools. Check against experience: think of a range of organizations you have belonged to since childhood. These could include Cubs, Guides, Boys Brigade, sports clubs, church organizations, bowling, darts, dancing, bridge – anything! Add to that list all the organizations you have worked in and for as an adult. Which would be the best of those organizations and why? You will probably be able to say with hindsight in which of them you felt motivated, well-led, or, simply happy. As a teacher or other worker you will certainly be very aware of those organizations or schools in which you felt prepared to give your own discretionary effort beyond your contractual requirements. Assuming that you *can* point to earlier experiences where you felt positive about your organization or workplace, why was this so? Our memory of childhood organizational life is always unreliable. Nevertheless, even quite young people are shrewd enough to sense when they are being led through a series of activities which have no purpose. A youth organization, perhaps, where the hard-pressed leader was following a handbook rather than a vision; the netball team where the niceties and technicalities of the skills coaching were pursued at the expense of a vision of effective teamwork; the vacation job at college where no one even explained the part which your modest efforts played in building the success of a wider enterprise. More recent memories, such as other schools where you have worked, will give even more telling insight into what makes an organization feel wrong or demotivating for you.

Vision makes a difference

Conversely, we remember the thrill of belonging to the team which supported each other in a selfless common cause (perhaps while losing most of its games!), the youth leader who, while not necessarily converting us to some noble paragon at least gave us a working model of something better and higher. At its simplest we responded as children – and we continue to respond as professional adults – to clear and purposeful statements about what our organization stands for, about what it believes in, about where it is going and about how our own small contribution is part of all that. Where these simple precepts are defective or absent we feel ill-led, ill-directed and on the whole disinclined to donate discretionary effort to the organization.

Schools need vision. Of all organizations, those dealing with the intellectual formation, skilling and nurture of young people need vision. No school can assume that its teachers all share common purpose, all espouse a relevant set of values and all articulate those values in their day-to-day work. Unless the sense of vision is clearly debated, regularly restated and firmly embedded in what the school does you might as well assume it is not there.

Vision, however, is not just a handy tool for the motivation and morale of the insiders. It is also the substance of the image a school projects to its user groups, its community, and to those with a stake in evaluating the quality of its outcomes. When parents talk informally among themselves about where to place their 5 or 11 year-olds, they may be discussing apparently tangential items such as uniform, rules and homework but what they are essentially doing is weighing up the competing visions of an education for their children.

What vision?

What does the term 'educational vision' conjure up? We have seen that it is about desirable and attainable futures and we note from our own experience of different kinds of organizations that the presence or absence of that vision contributes enormously both to the success of those organizations and to the individual's sense of well-being and motivation within them. Nevertheless, in schools we still have a certain discomfort with the whole notion of vision.

Part of our discomfort is no doubt related to a traditional distrust of charisma and fervour in public life. The thought of schools dealing in visionary sloganizing must strike a chill in many rational educationalist hearts. We find it hard to accept too many public statements with a visionary content and we instinctively fear the prospect of school leaders haranguing teachers, pupils or parents in visionary or ideological terms. We are also, of course, victims of our own memories of schooling in this respect. We may, for example, associate educational vision with recollections of headteachers and others droning on interminably about good behaviour, team spirit or the importance of homework.

So, vision is not about public rhetoric. Nor is it concerned with slogans. Is it then a lofty concern with the metaphysics of unattainable futures? A philosopher's version of a person's reach exceeding their grasp? As ever, a working definition lies between these extremes. Schools which articulate a vision rooted in obscure educational jargon or 'Educanto' reach nobody. Neither do wild-eyed rantings about hack ideologies of whatever persuasion. The vision of a school resides in the following:

- Those public statements and writings which refer to a desired future state for the school.
- Those statements and tenets which describe the particular nuances of teaching and learning which pertain in this school.
- Those plans and purposes which enact the school's future while specifically articulating what the school stands for.

So far so good – but surely every school already does this, already makes its vision explicit in its policy and practices? Not necessarily. Here are some examples of typical statements. They have been adapted from a range of school documentation past and present. In reviewing them, try to answer the question, 'Do these statements relate to a vision of the future of the school and is that vision clear and comprehensible to a variety of audiences?'

1. This school believes in enabling each and every pupil to achieve their maximum potential performance in all aspects of school life.
2. This school is helping to form future citizens with a range of skills, knowledge and attributes necessary to taking a full part in a modern and fast-changing society.
3. We believe in equality of opportunity in our school; all pupils have access to the full range of learning opportunities regardless of their gender, ethnic origin or physical ability.
4. We have a high expectation of all pupils; we expect the highest standards of achievement across the whole curriculum and individual levels of attainment are closely monitored to achieve this.
5. The school expects and requires the highest standards of behaviour and mutual respect from all pupils. Acts of violence and of intolerance are not acceptable, neither is any behaviour which prevents other pupils from learning.

Whose vision? The dilemma of participation

Clearly these statements range far and wide. When school leaders individually and schools corporately present these statements, they presumably have in mind an audience or audiences. If schools are following current advice on, say, school development planning then they are also involving some of those audiences in the design of such statements. This raises the first dilemma in trying to establish what counts as the educational vision of a school. Is it the vision of an individual (the headteacher?), is it the joint vision of the teaching staff, or is it the product of long consultations with other interested audiences such as parents, community and, perhaps, pupils? It may be some combination of all of these. School leaders receive constant encouragement to consult with their partners in the school's community. In doing this, you are generating a real sense of ownership and belonging. Unfortunately, a process of consultation and sharing over something as fundamental as the vision and mission of the school also needs a firm input from you, the leader. Other partners expect involvement but do not expect to drive the educational vision of the school: that is the leader's responsibility. Many schools have undertaken consultative processes over their aims and purposes. The purpose of this consultation and participation, however, is not to start from a blank sheet with questions like, 'What is our school here for?' Consultation in this case should be aimed at sharing and checking the vision, even if this means adjusting it in the light of those consultations. The vision begins with the school leader. There are dangers in defining vision simply by looking for the commonalities in the inputs of all the parties. If the vision is a 'committee' product then the following are likely:

- it will have been adjusted on a deficit model, ie, refined to *embrace* competing interests and to *avoid* offending any special interests;
- it will be expressed in broad and conciliatory language, 'a mile wide and a micron deep'; the statements reproduced earlier fall into that category;
- it will be difficult to audit and impossible to contradict. This means that you will never know how well you are doing in promoting and achieving that vision;
- it will resemble thousands of similar statements and probably be little different from that of the school down the road;

- it loses you the opportunity to be distinctive and special as a school;
- it will appear to apply to everything the school does but will change nothing. A clear and workable statement of educational vision should inspire change and progress.

Unfortunately, among publicly available statements of what schools stand for, examples such as those considered are all too common. Few are distinctive or special. Most of them bear the clear stamp of being the 'lowest common denominator' resulting from a process of discussion. So why are such relatively meaningless statements so prevalent and how can you get beyond them to something better? The answer is surely that the kind of statements reproduced above have in fact a quite different function. They are presented as the vision or aims or purposes of the school, but in reality they are analogous to the 'approved for vegetarians' sticker on a can of food or the 'conforms to regulations' tag on an electrical appliance. In other words they are there to reassure and to confirm. They present a baseline commitment to good practice and to common sense. They are necessary just as fire regulations are necessary. They would be conspicuous by their absence. They do not represent an educational vision.

Values and vision

Thus far we have a potentially depressing picture. Vision is vital (agreed). Vision drives a school (agreed). We look for vision in a range of available statements (agreed). We find a catalogue of lowest common denominator truisms and platitudes (agreed, but necessary). Perhaps a more fruitful way in is to consider the relationship between vision and values.

The importance of values, particularly those of the leader or manager is well researched and documented in the literature of leadership and administration. Hodgkinson (1978), Sergiovanni (1991) and others have variously asserted the primacy of values or indeed of moral precept in creating and sustaining a positive culture in organizations. Burns (1978), in emphasising the difference between 'transactional' and 'transformational' leadership, identifies strongly the role of higher-level goals, inspiration through ideals and moral questions of motive and need. Fullan (1991) ties this closely with building new cultures in schools, cultures in which clear values and vision play a pre-eminent part in moulding successful schools. It is no accident that most of the literature of leadership in schools and of leadership generally which highlights the terms 'culture', 'vision', 'values' and 'mission' is North American. Without suggesting that these sources are in some sense right or 'better' than British writing on the same subjects, they do display an energy, a passion and a fervour about building successful schools which leave many of our own precepts stranded at the starting line. There is a refreshing lack of embarrassment about discussing values, morality and culture, for example. That is not to say that the British do not acknowledge or indeed follow many of these precepts. However, it is this reluctance to deal with values head-on which acts as a brake on much educational endeavour. There is a saying about attitudes to change, for example, which goes;

> American: Ready, fire – aim, ready, fire – aim, etc. until target hit.
> British: Ready, aim, not ready. Ready, not ready, aim, not ready, etc. until target disappears!

Peters (Peters and Waterman, 1982), referring as it happens to American organizations with poor attitudes to change, called this phenomenon 'paralysis by analysis'.

Vision, values and competence

A recently developed programme which evaluates potential and serving headteachers on their leadership competences also reveals interesting insight into the values question. This programme, the National Educational Assessment Centre (NEAC) is building on 15 years of development work by the North American Secondary School Principals Association (NASSP). The British version, like the American, is using 12 fundamental leadership competences, assessed through job-related exercises, as a basis for the development of these potential heads. The 12 competences range from the administrative to the personal and they are not viewed in any hierarchy, ie, they are all seen as equally relevant. One of these competences is 'educational values'. The competence is assessed very objectively. Participants at these assessment centres are not therefore judged on the quality or rightness of their educational values but on whether they possess and articulate them or not. The UK project is still in its infancy at the time of writing but the early experience of putting 200-plus participants through the process (heads and deputies, primary and secondary) is that senior staff in British schools are on the whole reluctant to articulate important educational values beyond the low level represented in the sample statements reproduced earlier in this chapter. The conclusion is perhaps *not* that these senior and well-qualified and experienced educationalists do not possess educational values; those same educational leaders in fact demonstrate great sensitivity to value questions in informal dialogue. Rather, and importantly for this discussion, they find it awkward, inappropriate or otherwise difficult to *articulate* these values or to *incorporate* them into a range of tasks and activities typical of headship.

Since values and vision are so closely related, and since vision implies values, it is hardly surprising that so many school statements about mission and vision are so impoverished. It is almost as though values are unfashionable or as if they are dangerous or intrusive.

There are important lessons in this for you as the school leader. You cannot succeed, nor can your school succeed, unless you are prepared to be clear about the values which are driving the school's vision. You have to make the 'leap of faith' at some stage and make these important connections between values, vision and leadership. You cannot do this as a solitary enterprise or as an intellectual exercise. You will be expected not only to articulate what you believe, but also to interpret it for others. If you want your school's vision to be distinctive and meaningful then it must reflect real values rather than sanitized consensus.

Values are everywhere!

As we have seen, a major blockage in developing a clear sense of vision in school leadership is difficulty with educational values. Where these values are dormant, understated or avoided in some sense, then you must develop strategies to bring them out where they can be argued, defended and used to inspire the life of the school. Of course, values and vision are there in the repertoire of individual teachers and school leaders even if they are not surfacing in the kind of public way which establishes a school as having a special and important purpose. Certainly, when taking part in staffroom debate or in a governors' meeting or indeed in any casual discussion with informed lay people about education today, one is assailed by the plethora of values and value statements. Informal educational discussion constantly reveals individual values and clashes of values. Certain of these value clashes are beyond the ambit of school-level debate. If governments and others with a statutory stake in the process and outcomes of schooling wish to legislate, direct or otherwise order changes in schooling then they may do so. To oppose such change other than through the (admittedly often cursory) opportunities for consultation is to engage in a different level of activity which is essentially political. Of course much of the current agenda for educational change appears to many teachers to be grounded in values and visions which they find inimical; many educationalists hold values about teaching and learning which are in direct contradiction to what they perceive as being 'done' to them. What you as the school leader can do is to lead these debates by clarifying what is beyond the school's remit – and therefore non-negotiable – as opposed to what is worth negotiating. The inference for leadership here is surely clear; however regulated and legislated a school system may be, the scope for your school to be special, different and successful is enormous.

Vision and your school

If educational debate in schools really is awash with deeply-held principles and values, and if individual school leaders on the whole do possess sophisticated values about the purposes of education, then what can be done to articulate these debates more closely into the *public* image and presentation of the school?

Elsewhere in this book (p61) there is a discussion of the 'professional ethic' and its impact on the tasks of leadership. One long-established manifestation of the professional ethic is that communities of professional colleagues tolerate – and even welcome – wide differences of opinion about, and interpretation of, the core mission of the organization. Generations of undergraduates, for example, have noted widely differing and contradictory positions among their university tutors in the same department. It is arguable that without this diversity the very notion of a university is flawed.

In schools the differences of position between, say, a team of maths teachers may not be so obvious to the pupils. In a primary school the differing positions of teachers within the same year group who of course guide the *whole* learning of those 30 youngsters may be very obvious to parents and may even be a cause for concern on the part of the headteacher. We are poised on a delicate threshold here. No school leader will wish to dictate narrow and specific values; it is not possible – nor is it desirable. In any case, many of the values which inform particular teachers' positions on important questions are in fact latent and will only be revealed or clarified through conflict or crisis. However, where schools face large-scale challenge to their view of teaching and learning, and where they are required to be explicit about important aspects of policy then school leaders are faced with a dilemma. This dilemma could be summarized as: 'How much diversity of practice can we tolerate if we are to deliver the educational outcomes expected of us in this school?'

Values, diversity and practice

The dilemma is phrased above in terms of practice but of course the underlying values will powerfully influence that practice. Teachers organize and deliver their curricula in particular ways because they believe that in so doing they will achieve a desired outcome. Diversity of practice among the same group of teachers is generally welcomed and supported by school leaders if the outcomes of that diverse practice are acceptable. Two competing versions of pedagogy are able to co-exist where each has a satisfied audience or where perhaps they are perceived as different routes to broadly similar goals. Thus if two classes in the same school are following different approaches to the teaching of reading under two very different but highly competent teachers with differing values influencing their practice then there may be arguments for leaving well alone. The competing values about the teaching of reading might even, in this example, be seen as a strength if the outcome of pupil literacy is equally evident in both classes and if parents are equally satisfied.

A more subtle example of diversity of practice would be where two teachers take different approaches to fundamental matters of order and discipline. One teacher takes a stern and formal approach, correcting and punishing where appropriate, while the other takes a relaxed and informal approach, relying on the emerging social skills of the class to prevent or to deal with disorder. Each maintains the respect of pupils and parents alike; each achieves acceptable pupil outcomes; each is applying personal values to the building of a successful learning environment. Is there any reason to intervene? Perhaps not – unless this diversity has consequences elsewhere in the school. The school leader in this example would have a problem if other teachers in the school pointed to one or other of these two as hindering a common approach to order and discipline. Other teachers might argue that pupils are becoming confused and even rebellious because of the conflicting expectations aroused in different classrooms. Such a conflict should not be resolved by an arbitrary judgement or intervention by the leader. If the school has a well-considered view of order and discipline as part of its vision then there should at least be a point of reference by which the leader could address all the staff on such an issue.

The justification for tolerating and welcoming diversity in schools has always been that the overarching goals of good teaching, effective learning and care and control of pupils are more important than the detail of how they are achieved.

Modern school leaders unfortunately now have less choice in some of these questions of diversity of practice than previous generations had. Whatever your own response to the two examples given above, it now matters more that you can account for uniformity of approach over a range of teaching and learning issues. This may involve new and difficult challenges. A coherent vision and mission for a school implies a degree of uniformity on the part of teachers and in promoting an acceptable level of uniformity, as opposed to a rigid corset, the school leader will have to confront problems.

There is a dilemma for you in addressing some of these problems. The evolved professional ethic in educational leadership has led many school leaders into avoiding addressing certain problems. It has been argued elsewhere (Holmes and Neilson, 1988) that this avoidance consisted of a respect for problems, as opposed to a problem-solving approach. Leaders in organizations which have easily defined processes and outcomes are geared to addressing problems and attempting to solve them. This does not mean that they are braver or smarter than school leaders. It simply means that the problems which occur are more readily identifiable as problems than those which occur in schools. Where the outcomes of the organization are negotiable, debatable or otherwise elusive as is the case for most outcomes of the educational process, then school leaders are often reluctant to deem one approach as unsatisfactory or as failing. Thus, leaders in schools have worked in cultures where enormous diversity of practice, clashes of values and competing visions about the purpose of the school have been not only commonplace, but welcomed and even applauded. In this kind of culture you are very wary of promoting increased conformity in case it upsets professional sensibilities or provokes unnecessary conflict. All this is changing rapidly and the most important change is that the indicators of success and failure for schools are now largely driven from outside the school through demands for hard statistical information about every aspect of the school's life and the learning outcomes of pupils in particular. You now accept, therefore, that your definition of what counts as a problem, particularly where diversity of practice is concerned, is much sharper. School leaders are faced with the pressure to intervene at a level unthinkable a few years ago. To summarize:

- Public expectation of educational outcomes implies more conformity of practice in delivering the curriculum within the school than used to be the case.
- The range of allowable practice within discrete areas of a school's teaching, learning and care is narrowing.
- This narrowing of the range of practice may involve many teachers reconsidering the values underpinning their teaching. It may also mean school leaders being more aware of problems and being under increased pressure to intervene.
- There is still a powerful need for leaders and whole schools to articulate clear values and vision in a time of rapid change. Where outside forces are also guiding the school's destiny, the need for clarity of purpose inside the school is paramount.
- Any large-scale challenge to existing values and vision in a school leaves a vacuum which must be filled quickly with a reformulation or restatement of values and vision if the school is not to drift into a pragmatic and rudderless morass.

Building and sustaining the vision

We have seen that a sense of vision, mission and purpose is what binds a school together. That purpose is nourished by the values which underpin it. Values need articulating and challenging if they are to achieve anything. Values come under pressure in a time of rapid change and school leaders are in turn under pressure to be clear where the school stands on fundamental questions of teaching, learning and care. What are the processes which build and sustain the vision?

What is basic, what is non-negotiable?

The school leader needs to clarify for him or her self which of the school's purposes are non-negotiable. Non-negotiable purposes include a range of 'hygiene' factors such as maintaining a (literally) healthy and safe environment. Statutory requirements concerned with monitoring and reporting on a wide range of issues including attendance, outcomes of pupil assessments and financial matters are also non-negotiable. It is arguable that the non-negotiable also includes certain statements about pupils' learning, about care and support and about access to educational opportunity along the lines of the sample statements discussed earlier in this chapter. Most of these and similar statements are so unobjectionable that they could apply to any school in the country and could be accepted by virtually any mainstream educationalist or interested lay person. As we have seen, they also represent a baseline commitment to pupils' learning and care. So, part of your vision will be clear statements about these 'basics', even if some of them appear trite or clichéd.

Vision and change

Within the commitment to non-negotiable areas there is already the potential for conflict. What a headteacher sees as 'given' or in some sense 'required' of the school may not match the perceptions of other staff, or indeed of parents and others. Commitment to a new curriculum framework and to a particular model of testing and reporting outcomes, for example, will inevitably challenge existing views of what a school is trying to do, if only because they are new. The challenge for the leader is, 'Are these new requirements an integral part of what we do here, and therefore part of our vision; are they something to be domesticated and tamed to fit our existing practices or are they an unpleasant interference which we hope will go away?' No doubt in most schools *all* these views are held variously by different interested parties. The first duty of the leader, and particularly in a time of critical change, is not just to decide what is non-negotiable but to articulate it and to agree with interested parties how new demands change the vision of the school. Leaders will not change deeply-held values overnight. They do have a duty, however, to ensure that a critical mass of support and commitment is available to carry through the school's purposes. Their own commitment to change must be total once a decision is made. To collude informally with their teachers' philosophical doubts about change is dangerous. It implies that leaders will not be exercising full commitment and it gives an excuse for others to participate only partially. There is little point in managing processes which directly affect children's learning in a half-hearted way. If one aspect of the school's activity is perceived as being 'necessary but tedious', 'tangential to the core mission' or otherwise unimportant, then the school is sending dangerous messages to its audiences. Educationalists have indeed found it hard to accept that more and more of what counts as schooling is determined, legislated or otherwise controlled by other powers. This task, of articulating what is required of the school and of redefining the school's vision in consequence, is therefore not easy. Nevertheless, you must be prepared to restate, defend and refine your school's vision, mission and purposes constantly.

Practical strategies for sustaining the vision

1. Leaders should question themselves frequently and harshly about their own educational values and vision and those of their school. Have I understood how external requirements for change affect existing assumptions about teaching and learning in my school? Leaders should not allow themselves clichés about the importance of learning or the sanctity of the individual. They need to be clear what that means in practice. These thoughts should be written down and shared with those the leader trusts.
2. These issues should be articulated in simple terms to staff, parents, governors and others. Where change is coming, it is necessary to be especially diligent in explaining and debating how that change affects existing assumptions about what the school stands for and where it is going. Any written statements about school aims and vision should be reconsidered at regular intervals and at least annually. Comment on how these statements reflect reality in the school should be invited.

3. It is necessary to be clear about which requirements are non-negotiable for teachers, pupils and parents alike. Parents and pupils in particular should be told that the school is doing 'x' because it believes in 'y' so that 'z' will result. This means pupils doing 'a', parents supporting 'b' and teachers being tough on 'c'. Parents should always be invited to comment on the wisdom or effectiveness of what is being done, even if this means modification or change to the leader's purposes.
4. Leaders should welcome and encourage debate about values and vision in their school. Teachers are to be encouraged to articulate their own values, particularly those which influence individual approaches to curriculum and pedagogy. The values of individual teachers can still be respected even when those values are threatened or bypassed by change. Leaders should not be afraid to air their own doubts about change, but should not be half-hearted about pushing the school's mission forward where change is inevitable.
5. Leaders need to be punctilious about restating what emerges from processes of change. The new vision should be embedded in writing and in different places and teachers, governors, parents and others encouraged to read, hear or otherwise recognize those statements. Leaders need to ensure that no-one can be in any doubt about what the school stands for and is aiming towards.

The unchanging vision

The suggestions above are particularly focused on those elements of a school's vision which are new or which are changed by non-negotiable external factors. The commentary does not imply that any of these 'new' requirements are inherently good or bad, desirable or undesirable. Change *does* challenge existing values. Change is always difficult for teachers since they are dealing with processes which have long-term outcomes. Only a fool would pretend to guarantee that a particular change in, for example, assessing the numeracy of 6-year-old children automatically leads to more numerate 21-year-old adults!

Let us return then to those aspects of values and vision which most teachers would see as eternal, persistent or enduring. Whatever the legitimate concerns of governments in legislating or regulating the process of teaching and learning, the majority of what schools do is still largely the preserve of individual teachers in individual classrooms.

School leaders will wish to influence that through the exercise of policy, staff training, team building and the sharing of common goals. However, leaders still rely enormously on the discretion of the individual teacher for the delivery of the school's vision.

All the more reason, therefore, to clarify and constantly to re-examine those elements of the school's vision which teachers consider to be permanent and enduring. When the school as a whole, for example, stands by a term such as 'We believe in educating the whole child' or 'We believe in drawing out the full potential of every pupil', then these statements need a rigorous treatment. If they are part of your enduring vision of what the school stands for, then *every* teacher should be able to say:

- what this means for the whole school's approach to teaching and learning,
- how these values directly shape that teacher's own practice, and
- what evidence the teacher looks for to know that the policy is working.

These are tall claims. Is it too much to ask that teachers should be able to articulate the school's vision in their own professional practice?

If the school leader senses that this articulation is *not* there then he or she must act. It is not optional for teachers as to whether they can justify and explicate what they do in classrooms with reference to purposes, assumptions about children's learning and underlying values or vision; it is an obligation. In a successful school, in fact, it probably matters less what those purposes, assumptions and values are than that they exist at all and are properly articulated in practice. If vision without leadership is inconceivable as a route to effective schooling then leadership without vision is to rely so much on *ad hoc* and pragmatic rationalization that no planning for meaningful futures is possible.

Summary

If schools make statements about the quality of teaching, learning and care on offer, these statements must be meaningful to the teachers and must be explicit in their professional practice. They must be available to, and understandable by, parents and others with an interest in the school's success.

If the vision of the school's future is not being articulated in practice then it is meaningless. The life of the school must embody that vision and bring it alive. The school leader is the catalyst of that embodiment.

The vision can only be built and sustained by constant nourishment through the questioning of assumptions, through serious corporate debate about what is important to the school's future and through clear public statements about the links between policy and practice.

Vision, mission and the vocabulary surrounding these terms are often difficult and daunting for school leaders. There are many aspects of leadership where weakness, lack of skill or personal failing can be acknowledged but building vision and purpose is not one of those! Even if leaders are drawing heavily on the inspiration and imagination of others, those who look to them for leadership expect vision and purpose. Vision is therefore non-negotiable. It is fundamental to an individual's success as a leader and to the success of their school.

Chapter 2
Leadership and the Quality of Learning

The quality of children's learning is at the heart of everything the school does. This statement, or something like it, is regularly repeated in school literature. It is used by all the stakeholders in the educational transaction. It is unanswerable and undeniable. But what does it mean? How can you make sure that it means something in your school and that it does not become a piece of empty rhetoric?

The purpose of this chapter is to establish how children's learning is central to the role and behaviour of the school leader. In doing this, we need to consider a wide range of issues and challenges including how jobs and tasks are described, how structures and processes work in practice and, perhaps most important of all, how the school leader views his or her responsibilities for learning.

Defining the task

Putting learning at the heart of school leadership is hardly a revolutionary concept. From the simple precepts of common sense – keep your eye on the ball, stick to the task, don't forget where you're going and the like – to the more sophisticated models of educational change which emphasize vision and purpose, we have enough encouragement to remember what is important. In Chapter 1 we saw how the leader's own vision of the school's future needs to encompass a vision for children's learning. Unfortunately, as educationalists we are perhaps overelaborate in considering and in acting upon this encouragement. Because learning is so obviously at the core of the school's mission, we assume that the point is not worth restating. In fact, putting learning at the heart of school leadership requires action and involvement; it will not come automatically. Thus the task of leadership here is to organize the school, the teachers, the curriculum and all the attendant processes and structures so that learning can occur. As we will see, this simple statement is not without problems. How you confront those problems will determine your success in putting learning first.

Dilemmas in the task

Conflicting interests

Emphasizing learning at the heart of leadership may mean that certain decisions are made which cause conflict with teachers. The leader's view of what is good for children's learning will not always harmonize with the views of all the teachers. As a leader you are always endeavouring to strike a balance between delivering good learning outcomes and maintaining a healthy professional community with happy and well-motivated teachers. Since the beginning of mass organized schooling over a century ago, this tension between the needs of children and teachers has presented challenges for leaders. You cannot pretend that the tension does not exist. Every time you debate the issue of, for example, size of classes, you are engaging with that tension. Teachers as individuals, and corporately in their professional associations, are less clear about the tension. They tend to suggest that there is a congruence of interest between what is good for teachers and what is good for children's learning. Thus, improvements in conditions for teachers are assumed to promote better learning for children. To an extent, this is manifestly so since well-motivated and well-rewarded teachers will always perform better than demotivated, poorly-rewarded teachers. As a leader, however, you do not have the luxury of making this simple equation. Leaders in schools manage finite resources on which there are competing claims. Additionally, they are accountable for the outcomes of the learning of *all* the pupils in the school. Thus you will make trade-offs between different interests.

The dilemma of meanings

You will not need reminding that learning itself is widely considered to be a problematic concept. The word is used freely to denote a range of meanings from the mundane to the high cultural. A perennial source of conflict between educationalists and political leaders of educational systems is the dispute over what counts as learning. It is not the purpose of this chapter, or of this book, to define 'learning'! Nevertheless, an effective school must have a well-developed and sophisticated set of definitions and requirements affecting the learning which it is committed to delivering. These definitions will derive from:

- learning outcomes required by outside agencies
- learning outcomes expected by parents and other end-users (the next school, the college, the employer)
- the wider educational vision of the school
- the particular areas of excellence and specialization to which the school is committed.

The particular view of learning emerging from these sources will differ from school to school despite many commonalities dictated by, say, the National Curriculum. The leader's responsibility is to ensure that the view of learning is *clear, available* and *comprehensible*.

The dilemma of sharing

Thus the semantic problem of the word 'learning' need not detain us. What should detain us, however, is the need to share widely what is meant by learning in your school with all the interested stakeholders. Those statements about the quality of learning, for example, which appear in your school's literature must be accessible to parents and others. Not only that, but those statements must also be embodied in all that the school does. You cannot afford to assume that the debate about learning is an 'insider' educational debate. Your school's definitions of learning and of the processes which lead to it, must be debated with and constantly restated to, parents and others with an interest in the school. If this argument seems to gloss over the important meanings and debates associated with the concept of learning then that is intentional. A school's clients look for clarity in what the school believes in and in what it does with its pupils. They are quick to spot ambiguity and uncertainty. They are often angry about inconsistency where some teachers follow one route to learning which is contradicted by the practice of others. The phenomenon of 'trial by car park', whereby parents conduct informal but usually sharp and relevant evaluations while waiting to collect their children is well known to primary schools. If you are in a secondary school, however, be assured that this rigorous and constant evaluation of what you do by your clients is even more prevalent as their youngsters approach the ages where their life chances are being crystallized by their educational outcomes.

The purpose of this reminder is not to suggest in some crude manner that parents and lay persons generally have sets of views about learning which are in contradiction with and opposition to those of teachers and school leaders. It is to remind you that where your clients are well informed about your policies and practices, and where these policies and practices are authentic and consistent, then those clients are more likely to support you in what you do. By contrast, schools which mystify the curriculum, which communicate with parents in jargon, which are above all *unclear* about what counts as learning, are schools which deserve the criticism and lack of respect which they certainly receive. A school's clients will be on the whole remarkably generous in accepting a wide range of educational philosophies and practices. They will accept the validity and integrity of any number of educational innovations. They will welcome even quite revolutionary changes in the delivery of the curriculum. They will do all these things provided that the school:

- explains clearly what it is doing
- involves the clients in dialogue about it
- is clear what improvements in learning will result from it
- convinces any interested party that *their* child will benefit
- is consistent in its treatment throughout.

There is a curious but important and even uplifting implication in this. It is that parents care more about authenticity and consistency in how schools describe and deliver learning than about the refined underpinnings of that learning. Thus, it is possible to find neighbouring schools in the same area with similar catchments and similar socio-economic groups of clients where quite contrasting philosophies and practices are in operation and where both sets of clients are equally happy with their schools. In the same vein, it is possible to see examples of schools where the policies and practices for learning are politically, fashionably and traditionally 'correct', but where there is a high level of dissatisfaction among parents. Conversely, there are schools with a clearly 'progressive' or 'child-centred' model of learning which have the clear support of parents. As school leaders you should take heart from this. Amongst the confusing evidence about what is most effective in promoting learning, about methods and styles and about resources and curricula, it is clear that individual schools *do* make a difference and that schools where the first task of leadership is to lead learning make a very big difference indeed. So what can you do to promote learning to the top of the agenda in your school?

Roles and tasks for leading learning

A sense of proportion

In a very small school – say a one-teacher rural primary school – the relationship between leading, teaching, caring and managing is beautifully clear. The one teacher does it all! There may be tensions between different aspects of that teacher's role and there will certainly be pressure on his or her management of time. There may even be gaps in his or her coverage as they endeavour to be highly competent across the whole range of skills, competences and knowledge required for the delivery of the whole primary curriculum. What this lone teacher does not have is a fundamental conflict between a leadership role and a teaching role, between a coordinating role and curriculum development role or indeed between a pastoral role and an academic role. However effective or ineffective that teacher is in their small organization there is no doubt where their priorities lie: the learning needs of those children are dominant. In larger schools, however, and particularly in very large schools, modern trends in school organization often risk getting in the way of that simple and vital sense of priority.

School structure and the leadership of learning

We cannot avoid most of the complexities which go along with modern schooling. Large schools need efficient management systems and structures. Nevertheless, a legitimate question for school leaders in a medium-sized or large school is: 'Do our structures and processes and the way we allocate tasks and responsibilities represent fitness-for-purpose?' One thing we have learned from a century of research and theorizing about organizations is that large and complex organizations seem to have an innate tendency to revert to a 'bureaucratic' culture unless leaders work hard to promote alternatives. In terms of large schools, for example, new and expanded roles, elaborate policies and procedures and layers of referral can easily proliferate, particularly where a school is growing or changing in important ways.

As a school leader your responsibility is to promote the simplest possible structures and processes which can deliver the school's purposes. Otherwise, you are diverting valuable time, energy and commitment into servicing *systems* rather than delivering learning. In doing this you are up against a lot of organizational inertia. People with established roles and responsibilities do not like to have them changed. Schools are reluctant to abandon policies and processes, even where they have manifestly served their purpose and are becoming redundant. They prefer instead to create new ones on top of or alongside what was there before. Thus if you create a new forum in your school – perhaps a regular curriculum review group meeting – ask yourself, 'What existing process, meeting or forum should we now look to reduce or abandon?'

Senior staff roles and the leadership of learning

Take a hard look at the job and/or role descriptions of the senior staff in your school. Are they geared to promoting the core mission of your school, ie, are they about children's learning? If they largely concern issues and functions which are a long way from learning then you should worry.

Of course, job and role descriptions do not necessarily reflect the way people perform – or even view – their leadership functions. There is a rich seam of school management folklore concerning job descriptions and you doubtless have access to a humorous example in your experience. The Oxford Centre for Education Management conducted a survey of deputy headteacher job descriptions while preparing a senior management training programme in 1992. The survey showed some interesting contrasts in these descriptions from the 'minimalist' through the 'technocratic', to the 'incremental'.

Minimalist roles

These job descriptions were essentially about exercising leadership within a team and creating the role as the school and its needs developed. Such schools were clearly more interested in recruiting a good school leader than in the detail of the role to be filled.

Technocratic roles

These descriptions gave massive detail about a wide range of duties, responsibilities, tasks and accountabilities usually arranged around clusters of themes such as 'Daily administration', 'Leading curriculum development', 'Resource management', etc. Such schools had a clear idea of what needed to be done and whoever framed the descriptions at least had some sense of logic and order in viewing those roles and tasks.

Incremental Roles

Perhaps the most worrying job descriptions were the 'Incremental' roles. In these examples, you could imagine yourself dating a tree by counting the rings! Typically, one set of responsibilities is listed in priority order and ends with something fairly mundane, then the next line introduces a new 'big picture' issue, obviously reflecting the achievement and orientation of the second person to hold the post. Typically you could read the careers of three or more incumbents in some job descriptions. Presumably such schools were seeking to appoint someone who represented the best of all his or her predecessors. One deputy headteacher interviewed for a training package on Local Management of Schools (LEAP, 1990) revealed how an obscure requirement to ensure the repainting of room numbers on the backs of chairs had survived in to a modern senior staff role across the generations.

Leadership, role and change

Of course job and role descriptions will always be imperfect. In a dynamic school and, particularly, in a time of rapid change they will date very quickly. Many school leaders have come to see enormous benefits in giving senior staff tasks and projects rather than elaborate job descriptions. Nevertheless, whether a job is fully described in the traditional sense or described in terms of shorter-term tasks and goals, the important question is still whether that description is relevant to children's learning.

Tasks and responsibilities which involve working across a school, rather than down a clear line of curriculum or age-group identity, tend to drift in to senior staff roles. Look at some of these in your own school. The key words to check for are 'coordinate', 'liaise', 'oversee' and 'support'.

Many of these responsibilities are real and substantial. Many of them are elusive and vague. Many large schools have responded to the large-scale curriculum changes of the last decade (whether internally or externally driven) by allocating each new theme or development to nominated individuals and by rewarding those individuals in many cases with salary increments. Typical areas of responsibility here include information technology, vocational education, cross-curricular themes, personal and social education, INSET, profiling, and so on. If this is happening in your school, you should be extremely vigilant. On a common sense level, people in leadership roles can only handle a limited number of 'real' responsibilities at any one time. For senior staff, it is better that they have fewer and more substantial responsibilities than more and 'thinner'. For any new responsibility which you consider allocating to a senior member of staff you should ask the question, 'What benefits in children's learning will accrue from this role by the end of this year?' If you cannot link new reponsibilities to expected benefits in the core mission of the school then you should seriously consider either rethinking that responsibility or abandoning it.

As a leader you give many symbolic as well as concrete messages by your actions and decisions. If senior staff in your school are overloaded with administrative or bureaucratic functions – as opposed to functions which are clearly about children's learning – the symbolic message is that leadership involves tasks and duties which are a long way from what the school is supposed to be there for.

Roles which are about coordinating or liaising are especially difficult in this respect. What do these words mean? In practice they may largely consist of talking, meeting, writing and disseminating information. Never forget that however well this is done, it is not at this level which learning occurs. It is at the level of the individual teacher working with pupil, group or class that learning occurs. Senior staff are there to enable and to support that learning as well as to furnish the structure of resources, purposes and accountabilities within which it can flourish. Publicly available job descriptions and responsibility need to reflect that sense of priority.

Keep it simple: bringing leadership and learning together

In the conventional wisdom of successful management in commercial organizations there has for some time been an emphasis on slimming down or otherwise rationalizing what we have come to call 'middle management'. Tom Peters (1989; 1992) has eloquently catalogued this movement and given graphic accounts of organizations which were failing through a concentration of power and resources in functional middle layers such as planning sections, personnel departments and other service areas. In those organizations which tackled the problem, there was a concern to focus leadership effort on to those functions and actions which furthered the main mission of the organization. The efficient and effective way to achieve this was to push as much autonomy, discretion and power as possible down to the level of the individual working team. If this meant, in some cases, dismantling, say, most of the personnel department and making individual sections responsible for their own recruitment and selection, then so be it. Large numbers of modern, successful organizations have undergone something of a management and leadership revolution in recent years. What is common to most of those examples is actually something very simple: reminding yourself what your main business is and gearing your management and leadership effort to serve that business. In school terms, the analogy with leadership for learning is striking.

Leadership and learning seen from outside – how does it look?

Fit and misfit

What would a modern management guru say about the leadership of learning in a large school today? Surprisingly, perhaps, they would make many approving comments. They would note, for example, that most schools are very well geared to their core mission of learning. Most teachers teach for most of the time and most of the rest of the time is spent on activities and tasks which closely support that teaching. The guru might also note that there is a reasonable level of staff development and training to support teaching and learning, that schools do not devote excessive resources to 'fringe' activities and that there is a relative absence of bureaucratic structures and attitudes. The same guru would also note the high calibre and dedication of the majority of those in leadership roles. So far so good. These general observations would apply to most schools, but before we become too complacent about the generality of good practice, we would want to press that guru on the detail of how leadership is geared to learning in schools.

On closer inspection the guru might also note some of the phenomena listed below. To list them is not to imply that those 'misfits' are wrong, bad or unproductive. They do however represent examples of leadership energy and and commitment being potentially diverted away from the core mission of the school. If the examples of misfit offered below are familiar to you in your school, then you will wish to consider whether they are giving unwelcome messages about what is important in the school. The examples are followed by individual commentaries which should prompt you to think of ways forward.

Observation 1

Leading teachers (middle and senior managers) in pastoral roles where the distinction between care and learning is blurred.
Potential outcome: confusion about who is accountable for successful pupil learning.

Analysis and response

Pastoral and academic leadership. Most large schools invest a number of senior roles in the 'pastoral' area. Schools which promote a strong pastoral curriculum through personal and social education (PSE) programmes require clear leadership of those programmes. Such programmes when well led offer significant added value to the school. What is very difficult to determine is the cost-benefit of such investment. The cost is not merely the added salary increments of pastoral leaders but the opportunity cost of investing in one area of the school's mission as opposed to others. There are now large numbers of younger, ambitious teachers in schools who speak of making career choices between pastoral and academic routes. You should be worried by this. Elaborate career structures which are about essentially pastoral responsibilities are not only expensive but they also suggest that the 'pastoral' is somehow the preserve of a separate élite. The dangerous message here is that ordinary teachers need not be bothered with issues other than teaching and learning – the pastoral experts can deal with all that!

Remember that investment in care, counselling and other pastoral support is dangerously open-ended and you have to demonstrate what the limits are to that investment. Pastoral support for pupils in schools is also notoriously difficult to evaluate. It deals in many elusive moral and value areas and is easy to do badly. Therefore, if you have allocated roles which are essentially pastoral, you should be ruthless in defining how those roles relate to learning. The learning/care relationship in schools is symbiotic rather than distinct. Pupils themselves need to see that their teachers are concerned with both.

Observation 2

Leading teachers with responsibilities for courses, for themes, for issues and for resources.

Potential outcome: disproportionate leadership time spent on debate, liaison and documentation rather than on close support of learning.

Analysis and response

Leading learning or leading ideas? Our guru's second observation concerns the way senior staff in schools prioritize their different roles. The early part of this chapter covered the broad questions of structure, role and task. Where the curriculum is complex then leadership within it also risks becoming complex. The old notion of a subject leader or head of department, particularly in secondary schools, is attractively simple. Modern trends in the primary curriculum suggest that subject leadership will be a continuing concern for all schools. But what *is* the right role and orientation for someone leading a subject such as mathematics or science? It might be a combination of the following:

- to be an outstanding teacher of that subject and to lead by example
- to conduct the 'business' of that subject
- to be knowledgeable about the subject, to network with others in similar positions
- to act as a link between the narrow concerns of that subject and the wider mission of the school as well as the concerns of other subjects
- to take responsibility for the learning outcomes of all the pupils studying or following that subject
- to nurture, develop and lead other teachers of that subject.

In defining the roles of curriculum leaders in your school you will favour some of these considerations over others. You should be able to say which of them are working to promote effective learning.

If these are difficult questions to answer for leaders of something as relatively well defined as mathematics then they are even more difficult for those leading such imprecise areas as vocational education, information technology across the curriculum or assessment and evaluation. You need to be tough about the relationship between some of these responsibilities and the learning outcomes of the pupils. As a general guide, the more vague and elusive the responsibility is, the more rigorous the evaluation of that role should be. Set criteria for the successful furtherance of roles. Ask the incumbents to develop targets and to specify how their activities are contributing to the purposes of the school. Above all, do not let vague and elusive roles and tasks proliferate. If you have to have them, keep them short-term, rotate the post holders and review them rigorously.

Observation 3

Leading teachers spending quality time on relatively low-level administrative functions.

Potential outcome: the symbolic elevation of 'administrivia' into a leadership context: senior staff retreating into the relative security of administrative tasks and avoiding direct engagement with the core mission.

Analysis and response

Quality time – quality leadership. The third observation from our imaginary guru will scarcely have surprised you. It is part of both the folklore and the real experience of all educational leaders that their day-to-day practice veers alarmingly between the trivial and the demanding, the routine and unexpected, the crucial and the mundane. More personally perhaps, we all reserve relatively trivial tasks to ourselves as ways of unwinding, of breaking tension or instead of a coffee break. A textbook on time management, for example, might suggest that headteachers are paid too much to do their own photocopying or make their own tea but it may be precisely those mundane tasks which keep them sane in times of stress. Our guru's point about leaders spending time on low-level administrivia is not about personal time-management skills, important though they are; it is that in schools we are on the whole bad at prioritizing leadership tasks which are not directly concerned with teaching. Thus, one of the more obvious examples – happily now uncommon – was of deputy headteachers spending most of the summer term in secondary schools on that mystic quest known as the timetable. Since 90 per cent of the work of constructing a timetable, even in a large school, is routine, and about 10 per cent of it is about judgement, values or discrimination, then did it merit effectively one quarter of the year's work of one of the most expensive teachers in the school?

There will be examples in your own school of administrative tasks such as returns to outside bodies, responding to requests for information, premises management etc. where senior staff time is being drawn away from central concerns of teaching and learning. Why raise this here? All schools have limited resources at their disposal. Nevertheless, most schools now are in a position to make imaginative innovations in the use of senior staff time. Very small schools will never have much discretion in this matter. Larger schools are able to act. If you were truly bold and imaginative, how many administrative functions could you draw together and invest in a school administrator as opposed to a senior teacher? You may not be making enough use of information technology to meet the increasing demands for information from outside bodies. Perhaps you could contract-out some of your school administration. Even very small schools, for example, have found it cost-effective to join with other small schools in joint bursar programmes where a specialist spends a day per week in each partner school efficiently concentrating on financial administration.

None of these ideas is particularly novel in itself. What they all require, however, as in so many aspects of effective leadership is an effort of will to make them succeed. In being imaginative about administrative tasks you are of course trying to liberate the quality time of senior staff so that it can be redirected to the core mission. Where you are asking experienced senior staff to change roles and tasks significantly, you want their hearts as well as their minds. If your school really wants to get a grip on 'fitness for purpose' in the allocation of responsibilities then it must be accompanied by a proper debate about why you are doing it and a clear rationale for focusing senior staff time on core matters.

Observation 4

Corporate time in meetings spent on issues and concerns which are a long way from the core mission.

Potential outcome: frustration with meetings structures leading to individuals withdrawing commitment and energy from corporate activity generally: consequent lack of imagination and inspiration when learning *is* discussed.

Analysis and response

Meetings and learning. The fourth of our guru's observations concerns the business of meetings and other corporate time. There are serious messages for any organization about its conduct of those occasions where large numbers of staff members are gathered together to make policy, take decisions or otherwise further the mission. You must never forget how expensive such time is. Try this simple calculation. Multiply the number of people present at the next school meeting you attend by the average salary of those present. Now divide the result by the number of hours which those present would expect to work in a year (either based on contractual requirements or on an educated guess about 'real' time worked). This gives you a rough guide to the cost per hour of that meeting. The important question for you now is, of course, 'Was it worth it?' Now this is a totally artificial and, you will argue, misleading way of evaluating corporate time. You are right. Nevertheless, even if you dislike the facile calculation you must agree that meetings need to give good value for time devoted to them. The point of this discussion is not to reiterate the conventional wisdom of how to manage successful meetings. There is a massive literature on that subject already. The point here is that the business of those meetings should reflect the primacy of teaching and learning in the life of the school. Take a close look at the agendas and minutes of the staff meetings in your school. Is there a good focus on teaching and learning there, or is there perhaps a worrying domination of those meetings by items and concerns which are less relevant to your core mission? Corporate events such as meetings figure importantly in teachers' perceptions of their schools. Staff meetings in particular send powerful messages to teachers about what is important and what is valued in a school. New staff will form lasting impressions about how business is conducted from their first few meetings. Most crucially, meetings which are badly conducted, which are overloaded with procedural or administrative business and which are dominated by a few powerful voices are extremely counter-productive. We are all enormously sensitive to our time being wasted or otherwise abused. If someone metaphorically 'steals' some time from us, we are quite likely to steal it back unconsciously. The stealing-back might consist of skimping on marking, cutting short a play rehearsal or spending less time on preparation. Few teachers, conversely, begrudge time spent in discussion of vital and central concerns which directly affect the quality of learning in schools. In these matters, as in so many aspects of school effectiveness, you lead from the front. You must signal the primacy of learning by ensuring that learning has a central role in corporate discussions. Do not allow agendas to be clogged with peripheral items, however fascinating. Insist that such meetings concentrate on the main business of the school.

Observation 5

Successful teachers being encouraged into leadership and co-ordinating roles and effectively doing less of what they are good at.
Potential outcome: Devaluation of the notion of success for teachers: implication that leadership, administration and management are more valuable than teaching and learning.

Analysis and response

Promotion, career and learning. The final observation from our imaginary guru reflects a continuing and almost ritual 'moan' within the teaching profession. How can you encourage and reward successful teaching without losing some of that teaching talent to leadership roles and tasks which take those excellent teachers further from the classroom? Teachers themselves would of course like to see successful teachers rewarded in tangible ways, as long as this does not imply competition between teachers or threaten collegiality.

Outsiders, and many politicians in particular, tend to see the issue in a simplified way: 'Assess the teachers regularly and give extra money to the best few'. This discussion will not enter the shark-infested waters of performance-related pay or payment by results! However, the flexibility of school finance and teacher remuneration today does enable a school to create promoted posts for outstanding teachers without tying them to administrative duties or other leadership roles. The old notion of senior teacher was intended to do precisely that. Of course, to create such posts in an average sized school then leaves certain gaps in the leadership ranks which need to be filled. Having rewarded those teachers and given a powerful message about how teaching and learning are valued in your school, how will you fill those gaps? Again this is a matter of attitude. How people are rewarded and promoted is always closely watched by teachers. Rightly or wrongly, they will always be uneasy where promotion is given to colleagues who are perceived to be weak or otherwise lacking in their own teaching. This is particularly so where the promotion in some sense enables the person to lead the work of other teachers. Conversely, teachers tend to view positively the promotion of a colleague who is perceived to be above all a good teacher – whatever leadership skills or competences they may or may not possess! Remember what we are trying to establish: that the leadership of learning is the prime duty of the school leader. Surely then, you would wish to see leadership roles in schools filled by teachers who are knowledgeable about learning, who are highly successful with their own learners and whose leadership functions are largely about learning. Of course these are not the only prerequisites for a successful school leader. You want your middle managers to be good team builders, motivators, planners and evaluators. However, do not be dazzled by the technocratic vocabulary of management in this respect. The core skills of leadership and management are remarkably congruent with those of the effective teacher. Be careful not to imply in your school's career structure that teaching and learning are somehow gradually left behind as people progress through the ranks. In fact they should become even more important. Seniority should be seen as taking a wider and fuller responsibility for learning even if the teaching load declines.

Our imaginary guru noted some examples of school organization which might get in the way of prioritizing learning. If your organization is well geared to putting learning first, you still need good information about the practice of teaching and learning if you are to lead it effectively.

Leading learning – do you know what is happening?

If your commitment to putting teaching and learning at the heart of your leadership is to come alive in practice, you need good information about what is happening in classrooms. A depressing fact of professional life for many school leaders is how little they come into contact with the learning process. You may be familiar with the story of the retiring headteacher reviewing a long career who admitted that his promotions and his career progress were designed to put him in a position where he could make a difference, where he could truly enact his vision and put his beliefs into practice. The sad reality of that career was, as he told it, that he realized at the end of it that he had never been better placed to achieve his goal than at the very beginning of his career when he had real power to affect the learning and progress of those 35 children in his classroom. The more senior he became, the less he really controlled anything.

There is no reason to be depressed by this story! Except in the smallest of schools, where headteachers inevitably have large teaching loads, no one seriously expects school leaders to share anything like the same teaching as more junior colleagues. Nor should a career be seen merely in terms of power and control for that matter! What is vitally important however is that those in senior leadership roles have deep knowledge about the teaching and learning in their schools. No one would disagree with that, yet it is remarkably difficult to achieve. In large schools, leaders frequently write references for teachers where they have the sketchiest knowledge of that teacher's work. Even leaders who make a profound effort to be visible about the school and to visit a variety of classes every week find: a) that this is immensely time consuming and b) that the relative artificiality of senior staff visiting classes creates an unreal atmosphere in which little of worth is gained and indeed a perfectly effective natural rhythm of learning may have been disrupted.

Formal schemes of teacher appraisal, rightly, have quite limited ratios of appraiser to appraised (usually one to four or five) and in any case the focus of appraisal is largely the development of teachers rather than to make available usable information about children's learning.

There is a further problem for the school leader in keeping her or him knowledgeable about what learning is occurring. Ask yourself this: what kinds of learning outcomes or teaching practice are likely to be brought to the attention of the school leader? The average? The mainstream? The unspectacular but reliable and effective? Of course not. Where a fundamental matter of teaching and learning is brought to the leader's attention it is invariably an issue of either 'good' or 'bad' practice. In the case of bad practice this often begins with a parental complaint. In the case of good practice, more happily, it is usually an individual teacher showing justifiable pride in an aspect of teaching and learning. Isolated examples of good and bad practice in the classroom are no basis whatsoever for forming an accurate picture of what is happening in a school. The school leader needs a better level of information than this if he or she is to give a confident account of the quality of learning in the school to those with a legitimate reason for seeking it. This is no easy task. The formal outcomes of pupil testing, whether statutory or the school's own, will give a partial account. Visits to classrooms will yield some information. Teachers' own accounts of the progress of pupils and their plans for current and future work will also yield good information. Unfortunately this is not enough. All the above mechanisms have their place and their uses; for the leader to have the very best information, however, he or she must create circumstances in which high quality insights into teaching and learning are regularly traded in an atmosphere of trust and with a desire for progress and improvement. In other words, the school leader cannot rely on a conventional mixture of reportage and casual visiting; he or she must actively engage with the learning process.

Engaging with teaching and learning

We have noted that school leaders have great difficulty in obtaining accurate pictures of the range of teaching and learning in their schools. Where they can exercise real leadership of learning, however, is in the priority they give to teaching and learning in their own leadership agenda. Here are some simple questions for any school leader:

Do you encourage debate and discussion about teaching and learning?

Do you regularly talk to teachers about what they are doing in the classroom and how effective they feel it is?

Do you publicize examples of good practice in the school?

Do you encourage teachers to make teaching and learning the main focus of their team meetings?

Do you ever try to teach alongside your teachers, as opposed to visiting them while they are teaching?

Do you disseminate information about successful innovations in teaching and learning?

Do you deliberately focus staff training opportunities on to fundamental concerns of quality in teaching and learning?

Do you make time to spend with your 'average' competent teachers as opposed to your high fliers or your occasional problem teacher?

Do you communicate to parents a clear message about the importance of learning in your school?

Hand on heart, are you happy that learning is viewed as importantly in your school as it should be?

It is tempting to make assumptions when you are a specialist within a specialist business. If you glanced very quickly at the questions above you could be forgiven for thinking something like, 'Of course I/we do most of these things. Teaching and learning is our business, we live and breathe it, we are of it and in it!' Do not be insulted by such questions; they are at the heart of school effectiveness and at the heart of effective leadership of learning. Leaders who assume that simply because the school is staffed by qualified, experienced teachers who turn up regularly and complete their contractual requirements then somehow learning will be at the heart of the school's life, may be sadly disappointed. Let us therefore return to some of those questions and look at what is implied by them.

Learning and teacher talk

Implicit in the questions above is the challenge of focusing formal teacher talk more onto teaching and learning.

Of course teachers talk about teaching and learning a lot. In fact, they often make poor party guests when present in any number since it is hard to stop them talking shop. When teachers do talk shop, either socially or formally, what is it they discuss? The list is endless. In the current climate of large-scale educational change there is always a political talking point. In responding to the demands for change from outside schools, the particular impact of a particular change on a particular school is frequently discussed. Colleagues are an endlessly fascinating topic. The pompous or tactless senior colleague, the unfortunate private life of another colleague, the foibles and frailties of governors, the personalities and behaviours of pupils, all these – as are their equivalents in any professional organization – are fit for comment. Nevertheless, once you have discounted the obvious topics for gossip and casual comment, how much time do your teachers spend talking about their planning, their teaching, their successes and failures with particular learning strategies, their detailed use of learning resources and the like? Educationalists who by the nature of their jobs visit a wide variety of schools often comment on the different 'feel' of different staff rooms as evidenced by the topics of teacher talk in them. This is of course a dangerously unreliable indicator of anything critical in school effectiveness! It is nevertheless interesting when, say, peripatetic music teachers (who may be in as many as ten different schools in one week) characterize one staff room as negative, bitter or cynical about 'the job' while in another school the detail and the successes and failures of 'the job' are endlessly recycled with verve, humour and commitment.

Let us be clear that it is not the job of the school leader to spy on or eavesdrop casual staff room chat!

Some practical suggestions

How, even symbolically, do you signal a commitment to teaching and learning? You may not like all of these suggestions, but you may concede that it is actions such as these which give those important signals about what really matters in your school. What school leaders can do is set clear examples and agendas. In making time to talk with a normal competent teacher about what he or she is doing you are clearly signalling what is important. The first time you do it might seem a little odd or even intrusive. The second time it will be recognized as regular and if done with sincerity and authenticity it should actually be welcomed the third time around.

Engaging with teachers about their practice need not be passive or uncritical. Do not feel embarrassed about asking fairly direct questions about the progress of pupils, about pedagogy and resources or about the teacher's confidence in tackling new demands. It cannot be stressed too often that in doing this you are signalling what is important to you and to the school. In not doing this, you are leaving a lot to chance.

Sharing teaching and learning strategies

Invite teachers to give short presentations at staff meetings on particular lessons or sequences of teaching which they have felt to be particularly effective. Value these presentations. Lead one yourself. Invite teachers from other schools to do this. Send your own teachers into other schools to talk about good practice. Devote agenda time in meetings to the learning needs of particular classes, groups and individuals.

Developing new strategies

It is axiomatic that there is no one best way of teaching anything. After approximately four millennia of the use of writing and at least a century of mass education in the western world alone, we still cannot agree on the best way of teaching young children how to read and write. What do you infer from that? That we simply have not found it yet? That it is there but that we cannot agree which one it is? Surely we infer that the uses of literacy are complex and that succeeding generations will define it in different ways. As a school leader you will wish to signal that it is desirable to seek new ways of promoting learning – that teaching is not a finite business, that there are infinite ways of approaching a learning task and that experimentation is to be encouraged.

Encourage innovation; be tolerant of the odd failure; remind your teachers that however the curriculum is described or even controlled from outside the school, it is in the delivery of the curriculum that learning will occur. Encourage teachers to discuss and argue the delivery of their teaching as much as the content.

Learning in the life of the school

Within your school's unique culture, you will have regular events and ceremonies, systems of reward and punishment and rules and procedures which together make up that elusive notion called 'How we do things here'. Some of these are obvious and conventional such as prize days, merit stars, charitable fund-raising days and the like. Some give clear messages about the place of learning and others are more ambiguous. A system of punishments, for example, which makes a penance out of something which should properly be associated with learning, is giving a bizarre message. Doing maths or practising writing as a punishment is a strange feature of many school cultures. Of those events, ceremonies and systems in your school, how many of them are directly concerned with learning? You should celebrate the progress and achievements of learners in your school. Whole classes or teaching groups should receive regular public recognition of achievement. School assemblies can address learning and achievement as part of their agenda.

Instigate an 'alternative learning week' once a term or every year. This notion originated in a polytechnic in the 1980s. Every tutor undertook to try out new, innovative or otherwise different strategies during that week. Booklets were issued to staff on '50 ways of not giving a lecture!' Students and staff evaluated the experience. Such ideas are easily translated to a school context. No one would suggest that one-off events like this in themselves transform schools. Nevertheless, they do concentrate energy, time and commitment on the core business of the school.

What else can you do? The leader's own orientation to teaching and learning

When did you last reflect on your own beliefs about what makes for good pupil learning? When did you last seriously discuss changes in the practice of teaching in a meaningful way? More fundamentally, do you at heart see teaching as an art? As a craft? As a perfectible business? Does it comprise clearly identifiable skills? Does it require particular talents to do it well? Perhaps you harbour some deep-seated instincts about successful teaching and learning which are not in harmony with accepted modern good practice – or with practice in your own school. Perhaps you listen to your non-teacher friends opining about 'proper' education (in the old-fashioned sense of quotes and dates and theorems) and you secretly agree with them yet feel professionally obliged to refute them. Conversely, perhaps you privately despair of much turgid traditional teaching which you see in your school and you wish that your staff would try more varied methods. Perhaps you would like to see more imaginative use of resources and less reliance on test results as indicators of success and failure in learning.

These are not idle questions. Just as elsewhere in this book the importance of vision and mission in the school have been stressed, so the school leader's own orientation towards learning needs emphasizing here. If your leadership role has taken you a long way from regular consideration of fundamental questions of teaching and learning, then you should do something about it. No school leader can afford to be in a position where they do not share the basic language and meanings by which the professional intercourse of the teachers in the school is conducted.

You, the leader and learning

This chapter has made much of the personal orientation of the school leader towards learning. Of course, you have always valued learning. You have strong feelings about its place in the life of the school. You know also that even in quite small schools, the needs of different learners and different groups of learners can be very different. You know that stronger instructional leadership is often required for weak learners than for strong learners. You know also that one of the toughest learning challenges in any school is to tackle the relative under-performance of very able learners who have found it easy to be 'good', even when they have the capacity to be 'excellent'. You are also constantly reminded by both educational research and by your clients themselves that the mass of ordinary, average learners in your school are easily overlooked when the needs of the weak and the able are so strongly defined. You recognize, also, that in leading and developing your teachers, in being a sensitive manager and in building effective teamwork, you often sit uneasily between the needs of those teachers and the needs of the learners for whom you are responsible.

In defining and meeting the diverse needs of diverse learners in a school, you also have a number of audiences who observe closely when important decisions are taken. Your teachers are very sensitive to decisions which affect their own working conditions, requirements and accountabilities. Parents take a close interest in anything affecting the learning and care of their own children. Outside agencies watch closely for hard indicators of success and failure resulting from your decisions. In defining and following your own path through this delicate terrain, your own views of learning, of its importance and of how it is valued in the school will be paramount. The messages you give through your own actions, your public pronouncements, your decisions and through your own daily discourse with teachers and others will powerfully influence the culture, climate and 'feel' of the school. You want that culture to value learning.

Finally, remind yourself constantly that in schools, however much we value, nurture and develop teachers, what is important about any teacher is their teaching and the pupil learning which results from it.

Summary

The paramout purpose of schooling is to deliver learning through effective teaching. School leaders' priorities for themselves, for their senior colleagues and their leadership tasks need to reflect that paramount purpose. Complex organizations produce many internal tensions and concerns which can easily distract attention from this core mission. As a leader you need to give strong signals about your own view of learning if others are to value it as you would wish them to. Be imaginative about engaging with the business of teaching and learning. Gain good insight into what is happening in classrooms, not just by visiting them but also by encouraging constant comment and reflection on practice. Reward successful teaching and effective learning symbolically and, if possible, tangibly. Make learning the most talked-about subject in your school.

Chapter 3

Managing People in Schools – Building the Team

Most modern organizations value effective teamwork. Service organizations, especially those staffed by highly trained professionals, such as schools, depend even more on teamwork than hard product organizations. It would be a rare school leader who did not acknowledge this in his or her description of the organization. Yet the lack of effective teamwork is repeatedly identified as being at the heart of a range of school performance problems. Formal reports from external inspections as well as informal witness from practitioners frequently point to team dysfunction at a number of levels: whole school, department or section and senior management teams. There are many aspects to effective teamwork. From a leadership perspective, however, you will be concerned with the fundamental building blocks, ie, your teachers' own view of themselves in your team, their sense of motivation and morale and their ability to cope with change.

In this chapter we will look at the essential components of professionalism, motivation and change. Throughout, we will be looking for insight into how the leader can make a difference through an understanding of these core themes.

The professional ethic

To make real progress with the complex challenge of managing people in schools, we need to go back to a fundamental underpinning factor in educational organizations, that is the 'professional ethic'.

It is part of the folklore of personnel management that the true indicators of professionality for any group of workers can be described as an inverse ratio of the number of times the word 'professional' is used by them to describe their work. So, just as actors and other performers overuse the word 'work' – perhaps to disguise the infrequency of it for many of them – so many workers such as estate agents, cricketers, policemen and others use terms like 'professional services', 'a professional approach' or 'professional performance' in order to describe functions which might better be described as doing a job well and with a good spirit. Barristers and surgeons, of course, rarely use the word.

Teaching and, to some extent, nursing have long been examples of occupations with strong claims to professionality which are from time to time contested in public debate. Etzioni (1964) in fact described both these occupations as 'semi-professions' and pointed to a number of reasons for this, including the fact that both were 'feminized', 'unionized' and 'mass' occupations. These reasons would not count for much with most teachers, particularly the gender reference, but his indicators of 'true' professionals are more interesting for us. They included:

- access to specialized and discrete areas of knowledge and expertise
- a degree of control over entry to and discipline within the profession
- one-to-one client relationships.

These indicators are of great interest to the school leader coming to grips with the phenomenon of professionality. The third of them is clear: for most teachers the client relationships are in multiples. Despite the emphasis on individual achievement and progression in modern schools, most teachers spend most of their time dealing with large numbers of pupils. As to the second indicator, the entry points to the profession and the internal disciplines would indicate employee status since they are determined by the employers. The first of the three, the knowledge and expertise of teachers, is the most fascinating. Since, effectively, the consumers of educational services other than school children (parents, employers, governments, etc.) have all undergone an education themselves they tend to regard much of the processes and content of what counts as an education as relatively open to debate or at least fit to argue. Indeed, many parents in particular view their children's education in a very consumerist manner, not hesitating to ask, to query or to complain about anything from the nature of discipline to the detailed content of curricula.

Thus the claims to 'discrete and specialized knowledge' of teachers are at best debatable. So where, if anywhere, is the professional ethic of teaching? It is in fact buried within the detailed organizational practices of schools and, as we shall see, there are aspects of it which may work against effective teamwork in schools unless the leader can create the right kind of climate.

Features of the professional ethic

Individualized practice

The most obvious feature of the professional ethic to insiders in education is the relative sanctity of individual practice. Although the content of the school curriculum is susceptible to massive external pressures in the late twentieth century, although most teachers join in corporate approaches to designing the curriculum and although current phenomena such as appraisal and inspection arrangements will effect certain changes, the *delivery* of teaching and learning is still largely conducted by individual teachers with discrete groups of pupils in separate spaces. This is the reality of schooling just as it was a hundred years ago and it is likely to remain so for the foreseeable future. There are still large variations in individual teaching practice and many would see this as a glorious strength. One result of this relative autonomy is, of course, that it is uncommon for most teachers' work to undergo critical review by peers other than at the output stage (tests and examination results). This means that awareness of parallel practice in a teaching team is largely by inference or by self-reporting. It also means that any team approaches to fundamental matters of pedagogy and teaching style rely on the consent and cooperation of members.

Communication and meaning

A second feature of the professional ethic in schools is the ambiguity of much of the communication between leaders and others.

The language and meanings of any professional group are always interesting to study. Teaching and particularly teacher talk, are full of insider jargon, mysterious key words and professional shorthand. For the school leader who is concerned to build effective teamwork this insider language and its meanings are not a problem – you grew into them and understand them well. Where you often do find problems is in the obliqueness and ambiguity of much professional intercourse. Here are two examples of professional dialogue from teacher talk. Each has been partnered with a contrasting example from a different organization. The intent on the part of the communicator in each case is presumably similar, ie, to give a clear message, but as the commentary indicates, the meaning is not always clear in our particular professional ethic.

Example A

(Headteacher in staff meeting): 'I would like us all to be more vigilant about students arriving late for classes.'

(Hospital administrator to porters): 'Please start moving patients from ward to theatre five minutes earlier than published times as of this week.'

Commentary
Before you cry 'foul' at the unfair comparison, let us look at meaning and intent here. The hospital administrator presumably has a clear rationale to this request; perhaps theatre procedures have changed, perhaps a survey of travelling time has shown that the average allowed is insufficient. No matter; the intent is clear and it is likely that it will be effected by those responsible. What does the headteacher want to happen in this hypothetical example? Presumably there are students dallying on their way to classes. Is this all students? For all classes? Who is supposed to do something about this? How would you know if it was successful? The headteacher is speaking here within our professional ethic. We rarely give direct instructions to fellow professionals. We assume that if a topic is raised, then the professionalism of the colleague or colleagues concerned somehow takes over and the matter is dealt with. This is not necessarily wrong or even a problem, until the obliqueness or ambiguity actually provokes a misunderstanding or a dysfunction.

Example B

(Mathematics coordinator to colleagues in a memorandum): 'I would like us all to vary the materials we are using for tessellation. We are not making enough use of the newly purchased items in particular.'

(Head of product design in an engineering company in a memorandum to design section): 'We have some new software packages available for stress projection; I would appreciate some early feedback on their effectiveness.'

Commentary
Both of these are in some sense evasive. Both leave it to the discretion of individual professionals to take action or not, as and when they see fit. In the case of the design software, perhaps the 'effectiveness' referred to is a sharper and clearer notion; the worth or otherwise of the tessellation materials is perhaps less obvious. At what point is a leader in school actually directing a desired outcome as opposed to suggesting a course of action or simply raising an issue? As a school leader you should think about this very carefully. Ambiguity in communication is not only bad practice, it can have a deleterious effect on professional relationships. Assuming that you were that mathematics coordinator, how would you have phrased that memo? Or would you have chosen a different method of communication?

Clear communication is essential for effective leadership in schools. Too much reliance on oblique language is very high risk. Ask yourself this: how many times do I use (or hear used) phrases such as:

I wonder if we might...?

It might be useful to..

Could we perhaps consider...?

Perhaps we could all...

We should all make an effort to....

One useful corrective for anyone in a position of seniority in a professional organization is the thought that 'We are the people we used to complain about'. In other words, those actions, behaviours and ambiguities which you found particularly annoying or counterproductive as a new teacher are precisely those which you should watch out for in your own communication as a school leader. When you were a junior teacher, what did you think when senior staff raised important matters of teaching, learning and school culture? Did you assume that they always meant someone else? Did you perhaps see senior staff pronouncements as something of an *à la carte* menu from which you selected according to taste? How, with hindsight, would you have altered those communications to make them less ambiguous and more effective?

Different kinds of professionals

Individual teachers will have very different interpretations of the professional ethic in so far as it affects their own work and behaviour. As a school leader, you will wish to have some common understandings in your school about what is a matter for individual judgement and action and what is non-negotiable. Clearly many teachers are not only happy with, but actually welcome a large degree of direction and control from senior staff. We might characterize these as 'restricted professionals'. Restricted professionals display some or all of the following features:

- reluctance to engage in corporate debate about major teaching and learning issues
- over-concern with the minutiae of job descriptions and accountabilities
- deference to authority figures which emphasizes hierarchy rather than collegiality
- readiness to receive direction on curriculum and pedagogy
- willingness to accept arbitrary indicators of educational success or failure such as one-off student test scores.

At the other end of a spectrum of professionality we might find the contrasting figure of the 'ultra professional'. The ultra professional would display some or all of these characteristics:

- eagerness and over-willingness to engage in educational debate, risking what Peters called 'paralysis by analysis'
- cavalier attitudes to accountabilities and detailed job requirements
- significant lack of deference to authority and hierarchy with an over-literal interpretation of collegiality
- unwillingness to take direction on curriculum and pedagogy; overemphasis on the autonomy of the individual professional
- reluctance to accept *any* hard indicators of educational outcomes.

Obviously both these types are caricatures and few teachers would conform precisely to the descriptors. Nevertheless they represent both ends of a spectrum of how teachers view their jobs and your task as a school leader is to establish norms within which a variety of people can work happily and successfully. Both of the types of professional described are difficult to deal with. On the minus side, both will take up a lot of leadership time and effort. The restricted professional will need a lot of direction, detailed guidance, confirmation and reassurance. The ultra professional, on the other hand, will create unnecessary debate and perhaps conflict, will cause uncertainty in professional relationships and may find it hard to conform to corporate values and purposes. On the plus side, the restricted professional may well be reliable, loyal, predictably effective and good with accountabilities. The ultra professional, equally, may provide precisely that radical spark which a school needs in order to question the unquestionable. He or she may be more attuned to a number of quality issues in teaching and learning than their more conventional colleagues and their lack of deference may be entirely productive if it unfreezes an unnecessarily hierarchical culture.

Whether you like it or not, as a school leader you will have to deal with a range of definitions of professionality. Clearly most teachers fall into a middle range between the two extremes described. So what kind of professional culture do you want to nurture in your school? None of the above should be taken as suggesting that there is one, relatively narrow, kind of professionality that should be encouraged. Indeed, a mark of a confident and successful organization is the extent to which it can encourage and welcome diversity within its core purposes and practices. So, in promoting a healthy and productive professional culture what should you be aiming to establish as basic norms and principles?

A healthy professional climate – conformity, morale and motivation

As a leader, you recognize the subtleties of the professional ethic and you try to work with it rather than against it. You will also wish to act positively to create a healthy professional climate as well as understanding the world as you find it. The following sections summarize some of the desirable features of a healthy professional climate in a school. Each commentary is accompanied by practical suggestions about processes which might be associated with that feature.

Appropriate conformity

The constant paradox in the professional ethic of schools and schooling, as we have noted already in this chapter, is the tension between on the one hand wishing to encourage autonomy, experimentation and originality whilst on the other, needing to direct and control for the achievement of expected outcomes. Every school leader meets this paradox and you simply have to face it, determine your own orientation to it and deal with it. Appropriate conformity does not imply slavishly following a given rule book. It does mean, however, that in a successful school there are clear and firm expectations about the few central concerns which guide professional practice. It means, also, that there is a high degree of discretion allowed to individual teachers in the meeting of those concerns. Tom Peters (1982) has described this desirable tension as 'simultaneous loose-tight properties', where the central purposes and practices of the organization are tight and non-negotiable but individual members are allowed a looseness in determining their approach to them. The challenging part of this for you as a school leader is in arriving at an acceptable view of exactly *what* is tight and *what* is loose.

Leaders who are over-anxious about tightness tend to rely excessively on detailed prescriptions for everything from teacher punctuality to acceptable language on report cards. If you have ever worked in a school where a substantial 'Staff Manual' or something like it governs all these things, you will be aware of how easily these cumbersome mechanisms can fall into disrepute. This is particularly true where lines of referral are concerned, ie, who to see about x in the event of y occurring. Even in professionally staffed organizations, people instinctively refer problems to perceived problem-solvers, not to those who simply fill a place in a line of reference. Leaders who are not clear enough about what is tight, on the other hand, risk severe communications problems and the unnecessary diversion of time and energy in the marrying of problems with solutions.

It is reasonable to have tight and non-negotiable procedures for:

- anything affecting health and safety on the school site
- anything affecting the immediate care, security and well-being of pupils
- legal requirements
- minimum codes of conduct for staff and pupils

- keeping parents informed about anything affecting the learning and care of their children
- deadlines for pupil assessment and other reports.

You may wish to haggle over some of these items, but most teachers would accept them as reasonable. The looseness which might accompany them is harder to specify. Teachers will, for example, take day-to-day decisions about what counts as a safety matter and what does not. They also need a degree of autonomy in determining when an issue of children's learning warrants communication with parents. In these instances it is for the school leader to give examples, to be firm about the principle involved and to delegate accordingly. The 'tightest' item of all in any school is the furthering of the mission and purposes of that school. If that mission is frequently discussed, widely shared and regularly articulated in what people actually do in the school, then it will guide teachers in a whole range of individual approaches to achieving it.

Motivation and morale

The second feature of a healthy school culture which demands the leader's attention is the morale and motivation of teachers. You are already familiar with the age-old tension between getting the job done and looking after the team. In its various forms, this tension resurfaces in most modern commentaries on organizational behaviour in schools and elsewhere. Blake and Mouton (1985) rooted their leadership development work in this dualism between task and people foci. More recently, Blanchard (1985) has presented a more sophisticated formulation of the same dilemma through his work on situational leadership. Tom Peters (1989) and Rosabeth Moss Kanter (1989) both write extensively on these tensions in best-selling works on organizations and change. Most teachers will recall the work of Maslow (1970) and Herzberg (1959) on motivation, if only from the psychology strands of their own teacher training programme. What elements of this research and scholarship can you as the school leader draw upon in order to establish your own practices for promoting high motivation and morale?

What do we know about motivation?

This is not a cue for a substantial review of the literature! The psychology of staff motivation in professional organizations is a complex and demanding area of scholarship. At the risk of over-simplifying, let us look at some of the central cues.

Motivation and purpose

The first chapter in this book underlined the relationship between vision and mission and the building of effective schools. Organizations generally – and schools are no exceptions to this – do not prosper without a carefully worked out sense of purpose articulated in all that the organization does. Nevertheless, in trying to build a healthy and productive professional culture in your school, this sense of purpose needs to operate at the micro level as well as the macro. In other words, you need to look at how individual teachers are motivated by the overall mission of the school. Do not assume that the school's vision is as firmly understood, accepted and articulated by other teachers as it is by you and others in leadership roles. Talk to teachers regularly about what the school stands for. Ask them how school policies and practices are working for them as individuals and for the pupils they teach. Seek critical feedback. One of the folklore items from the conventional wisdom of marketing is that in understanding how a product or a service is working you learn more from the dissatisfied customer than the satisfied one. Spend time with those of your teachers who are critical or ambiguous about school policy and practice. Your purpose in doing this should not be to instantly convert or to dissuade but rather to listen and to understand.

Motivation and status

Professional cultures generally have somewhat flat hierarchies when compared with most other organizational cultures. School systems in the Western world are remarkably consistent in this respect. Most of them embrace a structure in which a very few staff are senior managers or leaders; another group holds coordinating or middle management positions, and the majority of staff are locked into a status/reward structure which primarily recognizes length of service, with modest reward for additional responsibility. In recent years, attempts have been made, particularly in the USA and the UK, to temper this culture with an element of performance-related reward. There are many practical reasons why a crude approach to performance-related pay does not work well in professional cultures. At a philosophical level, such an approach affronts a fundamental tenet of the professional ethic. From the empirical work of Herzberg and others to our own examinations of our consciences and experiences, we can surely agree that, barring massive changes in remuneration and working conditions, short-term financial inducements are *not* likely to affect motivation and morale in any meaningful or lasting way. Nevertheless, we would probably agree from the same evidence that a) status does matter to individual professionals, and b) reward, in its widest sense, does motivate.

Status is a very dangerous area for school leaders. It is easy for the person at the head of the school to engage in the rhetoric of the leader as humble servant, the leader as first among equals or whatever metaphor appears to bring you closer in status to more junior colleagues. In fact, in the author's experience, headteachers and school principals are remarkably free of status consciousness and are genuine in their rhetoric of collegiality. For other teachers, status can be enormously problematic. It is not enough for you to downplay differences in salary, working conditions and relative power and influence. Individual perceptions of status *are* affected by these. Above all, individual perceptions of status are powerfully governed by the relative worth felt by teachers. The leader needs to be clear in his or her own mind about these different manifestations of status because their own approach will set the pattern for others. The status of those who do receive extra salary, different (usually perceived as better) working conditions and discretionary power and influence is clear. The recognition, the valuing and above all the worth of more junior teachers is usually less clear. What signals do you wish to give in your school? The following are suggested as practical approaches to creating a healthy culture in which status is recognized but does not intrude on organizational effectiveness:

- School leaders should not defer automatically to status in meetings and discussions. Value contributions on their merits, not on the status of the speaker.
- Involve junior staff in high-status tasks such as policy reviews and evaluation exercises.
- Avoid wordy or pompous titles for middle managers or team leaders. 'Assistant coordinator of cross-curricular assessment and monitoring' may mean something to whoever thought of it as a title but as a signature on a memo it merely invites derision.

- Keep a close eye on who gets which work space. Teachers who always seem to teach in temporary classrooms, rooms without basic facilities necessary for specialist activity or rooms which are simply cold or uncomfortable will make obvious assumptions about their relative worth in your school. Senior staff with light teaching loads and comfortable offices, by contrast, both give and receive equally obvious messages about worth and status. If your school has a problem of unsuitable work places, then which teachers should bear the brunt of using them until improvements can be made? Junior staff? Inexperienced staff? Senior staff? You? Make your own mind up.
- Watch workloads. In large schools where the who-teaches-which-class decisions are made 'locally' within teams, departments or sections, teachers are very sensitive to their own workload compared with the rest of the team. It is not useful to pretend that all classes are equally enjoyable to teach, that they all require the same degree of preparation and assessment. Some classes are more demanding or even difficult than others and teachers who perceive that they are disproportionately assigned to such classes will also make assumptions about status and worth.

Motivation and reward

Rewards matter. As we have noted, tangible financial reward in schools is limited in scope and its desirability questionable. In a professional culture, however, rewards come in many forms. It would be cloyingly irrelevant to say here that virtue is its own reward or that the best reward is the sense of a job well done. Nevertheless, buried in such clichés are nuggets of truth about motivation and morale in organizations which should inform your practice as a school leader. Max DePree (1989) writes, 'The first responsibility of a leader is to define reality. The last is to say thank you. In between the two, the leader must become a servant and a debtor.' When DePree says that thanking is the last responsibility, he does not mean last in importance! He is reminding us that we do not necessarily recognize the worth and impact of our work unless it is pointed out to us by our leaders. His comment about service and debt is entirely appropriate to the promotion of high morale and motivation in school cultures. As a school leader you are constantly reminded that the delivery of your school's purposes is in the hands of individual teachers, however effective your own leadership may be. To serve those teachers and, consequently, to be in their debt, is the cue for the emphasis on the 'thank you'. In practical terms, you will generate these rewards only through a deliberate and determined policy of recognizing the contribution of individual teachers.

A fairly standard technique used on leadership training programmes when addressing the issue of motivation in schools is to invite participants to identify and analyse events in their professional lives which they have found to be particularly motivating or demotivating. This exercise invariably yields two main sources of motivating experience: one can be categorized as recognition/reward and the other as trust/delegation. These two dominate the lists of both motivating and, in their absence, demotivating experiences. It is inconceivable that the aspiring school leaders who join in such training have all been somehow psychologically brutalized by a generation of deliberately insensitive or untrusting leaders in their schools! Our inference should surely be that the presence or absence of recognition, reward and trust is a more powerful factor in the professional lives of teachers than is generally recognized.

Typical testimony from teachers would be, 'She took the time to thank me for the extra demands I had fulfilled that term – it made me realize that someone had actually noticed my contribution and that it meant something', or '...being asked to take that responsibility, and being trusted with the resource allocation – it showed how valued I was.'

Recognition and reward of this kind are vital, but are not simply achieved; they must be sincere and they must be appropriate. Any advice or nostrum about effective leadership can become irrelevant or even harmful if they become merely items on a things-to-do list: 'Must be more appreciative', or 'Need to delegate more'. Recognition of something as substantial as an effective teacher doing an outstanding job needs more than a casual 'thank you' while passing in the school yard. In a professional culture, people are remarkably sensitive to being patronized. Recognition by the school leader should show awareness of what has been done and knowledge both of the effort involved and of the impact on what the school is trying to achieve. Thus, thanking a teacher for the quality of their report writing, and mentioning the impact of that quality on the parents receiving the reports is much more powerful than a routine 'thank you' for meeting a deadline.

There is much to say about motivation and morale in the context of effective teams in schools. The core skills of leadership are very much about dealing with people and in striking that delicate balance between meeting their needs and extending their horizons. In becoming a better motivator of people in your school you will do a few quite simple things, but you will do them persistently and rigorously:

- recognize achievement in an authentic manner
- relate the efforts of individual teachers to the wider purposes of the school
- do not be naive about status and reward – these things matter and your staff look to you for clarity and consistency in applying them
- establish your own criteria for determining the level of morale amongst teachers and check on them regularly
- never forget what motivates *you* and don't assume that you are unique in this!

People and change

The third dimension of an appropriate and healthy approach to leading people in schools is that of change. The literature on educational change is vast and growing. If change is the normal state of schools and schooling (since schooling is a manifestation of and is moulded by a changing society) then the rate and scale of change in schools in the late twentieth century is certainly abnormal. Further, since the source of change is now in large part external to the school, the nature of the management of change in schools is now vastly different. If 20 years ago curriculum change, for example, was seen as an exciting and challenging business which was largely a motivating experience for those involved, then with hindsight we can safely suggest that this was due to the degree of control which individual schools had over the nature and direction of the curriculum.

As a school leader you are constantly engaged with change to the extent that it is virtually your whole professional life. Unfortunately, your fellow teachers a) do not necessarily share your commitment to change, and b) are not as accountable for the outcomes of externally promoted change as you are. As if this were not enough of a challenge, you will also be aware from your own experience of change in a variety of contexts that individual attitudes to and perceptions of change are immensely complex. Machiavelli characterized change as the most difficult task of the leader. Before we become overwhelmed by the phenomenon of change, however, we should remind ourselves that most school leaders *do* cope with change most of the time; that most professionals have an enormous capacity for dealing with planned change, provided that it is well managed, and that the only alternative to managed change is unmanaged change – and that way lies madness!

No school leader can create a culture in which every conceivable change will work successfully. We can at least be certain that effective leaders do create climates in which change is manageable and where individual teachers can feel reasonably comfortable with change for most of the time.

Creating the right climate for change

The natural human impulse is to resist change. It is rare for people generally, and especially in complex and demanding professions, actually to welcome change. As a school leader you should therefore assume that the difficult part of educational change is not the desire for betterment which is presumably at the heart of all educational change, but the actual doing of it.

As a leader, you are always going to be closer to the sources of change than your teachers are. The powerful reasons why something must happen are much more powerful for you, because you are closer to the accountabilities, than they are for those who are a long way from those accountabilities. You do not create a healthy climate for educational change by reminding teachers that you the leader are accountable for such and such outcome to such and such body! Ideally you want all the teachers in a school to feel accountable for the outcomes of change. Perhaps your first responsibility as leader then is, in DePree's (1989) terms, to 'define reality'. Teachers need to feel that change, particularly where it is affecting the detail of their own practice, is part of a wider plan, purpose or reality and not an *ad hoc* addition.

Thinking strategically and sharing strategy

If you have done the hard work of establishing, sharing and promoting the vision, mission and purposes of the school, you have already created a climate in which change can at least be discussed within a rational framework. Unfortunately, this is not enough when creating the climate for successful change: you also need strategy. This is the difference between knowing what the school stands for and knowing what areas of change and development are likely in the next term or year. School leaders think strategically for much of the time. They network with other leaders, they read policy documents, they follow political debate and they seek strategic information likely to affect their schools. Their antennae are sharp and pick up signals and nuances all the time. Above all, school leaders – unlike the majority of teachers – have easy access to strategic information and the time, since it is expected of them, to make sense of it and to relate it to the needs and future of the school. What can you do to bridge this gap? First, you must share strategic thinking and you must do it coherently. Teachers are aware of broad political issues affecting schools but they are not always aware of how it will affect them at a level of detail. Make time in your regular communication with colleagues to interpret wider policy issues. Stay ahead of change by painting pictures of different futures which might affect the school. You might visualize this as a sequence of images or outline scenarios which become more blurred as they recede into the future. The medium-term is perhaps a pair of sketches with some detail and some hazily defined shapes. The sharpest image is what is going to affect the school in the next few weeks and months. You do not have to be a visionary in order to paint these pictures, you merely have to translate the flow of strategic information with which you deal into some alternatives for discussion and reference. You can never share enough strategic information. Do not assume that teachers have 'too much else to do' or 'have other concerns'. In regularly sharing strategic thinking, you are preparing a backcloth against which change is understood.

Planning change

Assuming that major change in your school is taking place against a background of a clear overall mission and a lot of shared strategic thinking, your next priority is to plan change in such a way that teachers are working with you for the best possible outcomes. As with most conventional wisdom in management and leadership, planning for change as a rational process is mainly common sense writ large.

Nevertheless it is remarkable how much change and innovation in schools suffers from poor planning and how many excellent ideas founder as a result. The following sections are not necessarily a sequential to-do list for dealing with change, rather they are a reminder of the features of planning which determine success or failure.

Have a plan!

Your school is facing a major curriculum change affecting most teachers and with implications for assessment as well as the detail of teaching and learning. The groundwork has been laid through sharing the strategy and relating it back to the main purposes of the school. Simply to describe the desired future state implied by these changes, while vital in itself, is not enough. Without swamping colleagues with paperwork you have to ensure that everyone concerned knows:

- what will change and when
- who is responsible for what in the change process
- what the resource implications are
- how all this affects them personally
- how they will know how the changes are working – or not!

Assume resistance

You do not have to assume stubborn defiance or subversive action in the face of change, but you should assume that however effective the groundwork, some teachers will have problems with change. Resistance to change is rarely due to pure conservatism. In professional organizations individual problems with change are usually related to one of these factors;

'I feel unsure about my skill/competence in carrying through this change.'

'I fear that this change will complicate or increase my workload.'

'This change affects my professional territory – I like this space and I do not want to share it/change it.'

'This change threatens my status – I feel that if it happens, I will have less worth in the school, less influence and that my career will be affected as a result.'

'Despite all the discussion and rationalizing, I still fundamentally disagree with what we are doing. My principles are in direct conflict with this change.'

Of course, teachers rarely use such direct language in discussing change. These sentiments will be the underlying reason, however, for much apparently illogical or unreasonable resistance to change. Check against your own experience. Think of circumstances in your own professional life where you have had a problem with change. Were you always confident and assertive enough to articulate the real reasons for your opposition to what was proposed? Or, (heaven forfend) were you ever tempted to engage in an educationalist discussion about why the change was undesirable when you really were more concerned with your status, or any of the other issues raised in the list above?

This is not an area where the school leader can afford to sit grimly on the high moral ground and dismiss the concerns above as peripheral or irrelevant. Status *does* matter to individuals. Territory *is* important. Feelings of being de-skilled or incompetent are painful and destructive as well as being enormously difficult to articulate or to share with colleagues. Workloads weigh heavily on people who already feel themselves stretched to the limits of their ability to do a good job. Therefore, in planning for change you will be alert to all these complicating factors. In raising, say, the territory issue yourself, you will at least furnish a context in which it can be discussed seriously and not kept hidden for fear of ridicule.

The most potent of the examples given above will be that of teachers opposing by virtue of principle, belief or conscience what is proposed. As a school leader you can only go so far in addressing deep-seated personal opposition to change. What you *can* hope and plan for is a climate in which these deep-rooted matters of principle can be openly aired. What should matter to you is that in planning and discussing change, you are all talking the same language, ie, not wasting valuable corporate time addressing a phoney problem because the real one cannot be raised. You will always respect a matter of conscience. Ultimately, whatever the underlying problems that individual teachers have with educational change in schools, they have to live with change and be part of it. You can ease many of these likely problems with change through your own planning and management of it.

Sustaining change

Your planning of change has been systematic and careful. The process of implementation is widely understood and those teachers who have any of the problems with change discussed above have been able to air them. What else do you need to give the best chance of a good outcome?

Sustain your own political will. Once the planning is done, it is likely that your own planning and thinking energy has been reinvested in the next major item on your leadership agenda. Meanwhile, as is the way of things, the teachers are about to start the hard work of implementing change. This is a dangerous time for you. Although you may not feel like it, now is the time to invest a lot of person-time in this change. Particularly where change involves teachers in new methods and new resources, the early stages of a change process are where success or failure are in the balance. Talk to everyone involved. Ask how it is going and do not take 'fine' for an answer. Seek out problems. Remind teachers what is at stake and give generous thanks where progress is clear. Remind yourself why you are doing this and where it fits in the future of the school.

Design and apply criteria for success or failure

How would you know how well (or otherwise) the change was going? It is tempting to deal with some orders of change in schools in a fairly peremptory manner. Where an external requirement is made and compliance is non-negotiable, most leaders will instinctively feel less committed to that change than where they are planning change from within the school. Inevitably, you will see your agenda for change as a hierarchy where some issues have a low priority. Nevertheless, where change is directly linked with your core mission as a school, the quality of teaching and learning, then you need some reasonably solid indicators of relative success or failure. As educationalists we prefer success criteria to failure criteria. We would rather be looking at the positive characteristics of change than the negative. Therefore in looking at the 'how did we do' questions of change we would prefer...

> This change will have been successful if the following (positive) outcomes are observed.

to

> This change will have failed if the following (negative) outcomes are observed.

Unfortunately, perhaps, a concentration on success criteria rather predisposes us to deem success even where the evidence is unclear. Here is an example. You are implementing a change in assessment procedures with one year group in the school. The teachers involved agree three positive outcomes which are envisaged and which you will look for in evaluating the change. One of these outcomes occurs, one sort-of occurs and the third simply doesn't materialize. Is this mainly a success? Half a success? Of course you would have weighted the outcomes differently – the first, successful one might outweigh the other two ambiguous ones. A much tougher approach is to design one or more failure criteria, ie, to describe a circumstance, an event or a set of data perhaps which would deem the change *not* to have worked. Failure criteria are difficult to describe and, psychologically, uncomfortable. They do sharpen your thinking, however, and force you to be clear about where the change is taking you.

Evaluate change and learn from it

As the discussion about success and failure criteria indicated, we are reluctant to be over-critical about change in schools. Perhaps because teachers invest so much energy and time in moving teaching and learning forward, school leaders find it uncomfortable to risk having that investment deemed a waste. As a leader you have to be rigorous about learning from those planned changes you lead. You want your school to improve as a result of change. Therefore you want to get better at managing change. You need to ask hard questions about what has been achieved. You must invite comment and, if necessary, criticism about how change is managed. Was there enough lead time? Were the expectations clear? Were there resource problems? Did you get enough support from me and from other senior staff? What might we have done differently? What have we learned and how will this improve our performance as a team next time? Do not fear discussing failure. If the evidence suggests that a particular change went badly or did not achieve its purposes, then spend time looking at that failure with those involved. Organizations which punish corporate failure discourage innovation and creative energy. You spend time learning from the failure of the project, not on blaming individuals for that failure.

Just as we have problems with the notion of failure in managing change in schools, we are also tempted to forget success. This discussion of change began with the difficulties and problems. Where schools succeed with planned change, as they do for much of the time, this success needs recognition, reward and reinforcement. Remind teachers of what has been achieved, thank them for the discretionary effort given and, always, remember to link what has been achieved with those wider purposes and values of the school which guide the work of every teacher.

Summary

Managing people as individuals, building an effective team and, at the same time, remaining focused on what your school is trying to achieve, represent a delicate balancing act. This chapter has only addressed a fraction of that agenda. It has concentrated on getting the professional climate right, on understanding the professional ethic and on dealing effectively with change. Much has been made of providing the right kind of motivation for teachers. Through all your dealings with people as a school leader your own attitude and the messages it gives will always be studied closely. Those who look to you for leadership will be very alive to ambiguity, to hypocrisy and to lack of rigour. Teachers will be amazingly tolerant of errors, of wrong judgements and of administrative shortcomings. They find it hard to forgive leaders who are insincere, uncaring or who lack courage in facing problems. It is now accepted wisdom that the principal competences and skills deployed by leaders can be acquired and developed to a greater or lesser extent. Behaviours can change; personalities on the whole do not. In accepting this, you should therefore seek to know as much about yourself as a leader as you possibly can. Find out where your strengths and weaknesses are and be very aware of them.

Chapter 4

Critical Dilemmas in School Leadership

Introduction

In most conventional organizations, including schools, leadership often appears to be characterized by intermittent challenges, crises and dilemmas, the outcomes of which determine the future development of the organization. However successful the school leader is in shaping the future, in pursuing the core mission and in building effective teams, it is these unforeseen dilemmas which seem to command his or her attention. In this chapter we will look at four clusters of such dilemmas. The four themes covered are standards, quality, resource use and difficult people. In following these dilemmas and in working out your own approach to them you will be aware of the problem of perspective, ie, they can look very different depending on where you stand. Most school leaders, like most people, are more comfortable in dealing with problems when they have a degree of control over the elements of those problems. Thus it is easier to deal with an open-ended dilemma such as the allocation of a new resource than with a closed dilemma such as the re-allocation of an existing resource. In people-management the same is true: it is easier to set out a programme of staff development for future needs than to solve a problem of underperformance in meeting existing needs. As a leader you are concerned to develop a leader's perspective on organizational dilemmas. The leader's stance, as we will see, is often different from that of others in the organization. Thus we need to tease out a way of viewing problems which embraces that difference but which also gives practical and feasible options for progress.

Dilemmas, problems and purposes

So far in this book we have stressed how powerful a clear sense of mission and purpose can be in enabling effective leadership. Where the purpose of the organization is unclear, ambiguous or open to debate, then what counts as a dilemma becomes a problem in itself. In other words, if you cannot get agreement on what the organization is trying to achieve then how do you get agreement on what is standing in the way of achieving it?

If the organization is geared towards producing a clear outcome (publishing books which sell, manufacturing toys, generating electricity) then most problems (books are not selling, toys are faulty, electricity blackouts) are traceable back to the core mission of the organization and have, if not easy answers, at least options to follow. In fact, in many conventional organizations true dilemmas (make this toy or that toy) are relatively simple sub-sets of the main mission: sell toys. School leadership is of course immensely complicated by the needs, aspirations and definitions of the stake-holders and interested groups surrounding the school. An apparently simple dilemma can have complex ramifications which outsiders find difficult to understand. Schools find it easy to achieve consensus on simple aims and broad purposes; detailed policy, however, is always open to debate and disagreement. The following matrix matches three standard school aims or policies with two measures: first (vertical axis) how complex is that aim and second (horizontal axis) how easy it is to gain agreement on that aim.

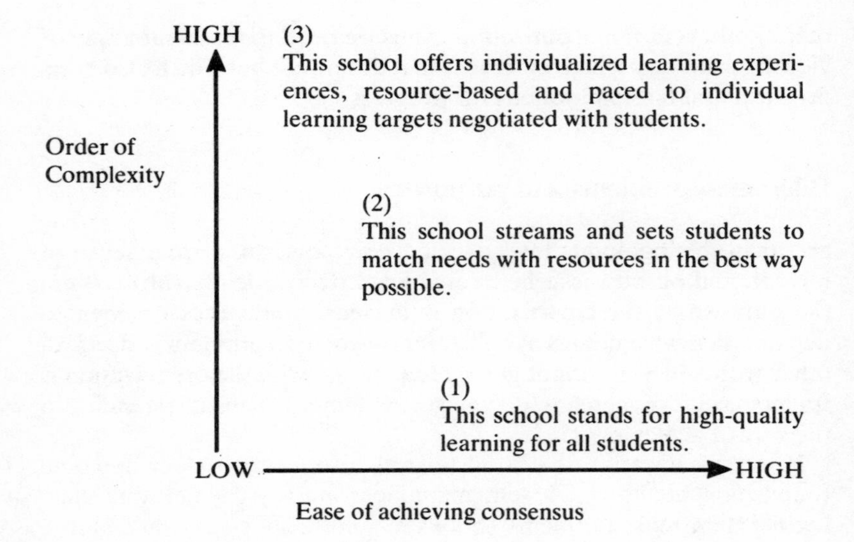

Aim 1 is vacuous enough to appeal to anyone who understands it. It sells itself by its simplicity. It is also, of course, meaningless unless accompanied by real hard processes which interpret and enact it.

Aim 2 will always sell itself to those consumers who see themselves as beneficiaries of the policy – and since they are likely to be more vociferous than those who do not see themselves as beneficiaries then consensus is relatively easy but is nevertheless still a problem.

Aim 3 is an 'insider' educationalist statement which subsumes a mass of technical insight and specialist processes. Consumers will need to have it explicated and 'sold' to them and even then may have reservations. It is a complex idea and even experienced teachers would not all view it in the same way.

Defining dilemmas

The school leader, then, has a number of audiences who will view his or her dilemmas in different ways. Relatively few of these audiences ever seriously query the validity of 'educationalist' decisions about curriculum and learning. The one audience which will always debate these decisions is the insider audience: the teaching staff of the school. As we have already seen, the professional culture in schools actually welcomes that debate. In the current climate of educational change, many issues which in a pure educational sense are dilemmas are, from a leadership perspective, non-negotiable. Where this is so, the dilemma is about implication, not about principles. One essential task of leadership therefore is to define clearly for all the appropriate audiences what is negotiable and what is not.

The dilemmas which follow represent a range of leadership challenges. They are offered partly as illustrations of difficult choice areas, partly as starting points for viewing your own actions and partly as a way of dealing with issues which do not always neatly fit the usual categories of leadership literature. Much of the commentary on these dilemmas draws on both the real experiences and considered judgement of the many school leaders who have worked with the author on leadership and management development programmes.

Standards

City High School

City High School is not yet in crisis but very soon could be. An external evaluation/inspection identified the following audit of strengths and weaknesses:

Strengths:
An experienced, mature staff group.
Prudent budgeting, adequate learning resources.
A stable pattern of student recruitment.
Excellent sporting and cultural facilities.
A coherent philosophy and mission for the school.
High quality pastoral and counselling services.

Weaknesses:
Poor and declining student achievement scores.
Insufficient diversity of teaching methods.
Generally unacceptable standards of student literacy.
An ineffective departmental structure.
Inadequate mechanisms for curriculum development.
Little effective monitoring and evaluation at whole school level.

Commentary

First thoughts

All case studies are flawed with a problem of evidence so let us not get caught up in a debate about the detailed meanings in the audit above. Put yourself in the position of the newly appointed principal of City High School. Consider the essential dilemma. It might be phrased thus:

> 'A well resourced and stable school is failing to deliver an appropriate quality of learning to its clients.'

or

> 'How can this school redirect its energies into raising standards of student achievement without compromising its other areas of strength?'

or, indeed

> 'The conditions for effective schooling are all present: this school is suffering from a failure of leadership.'

Already we see the difficulty of defining the problem. Remember, however, that we are looking at City High from a leadership perspective, not from the perspective of disinterested researchers or educational commentators.

Second thoughts

Clearly we might have difficulty even defining the nature of the problem. In fact a detailed analysis of the same apparently factual evidence would produce different interpretations when viewed from the perspectives of different interest groups.

One implication of the audit, for example, is that the staff have low expectations of student achievement. One response to this from staff might well be to formulate a sophisticated argument thus:

a. 'The outcomes criticised (student attainment) refer to one aspect of our mission. We have other, equally valid purposes in our school as reflected in our (praised) mission statement.'
b. 'The technical exercise of improving audited student attainment is not difficult. We simply direct time and resources into the preparation for and execution of the tests. We do not, however, see this as educationally desirable.'
c. 'Literacy is susceptible to multiple definitions. External audits do not appreciate the complexity and subtlety of *our* definitions of literacy.'

All of these positions are arguable and can be reasoned with reference to mainstream educational research. From a leadership perspective, however, certain things may appear non-negotiable. The most fundamental of these may be that if important external audiences identify a major shortcoming in our school, we must address that shortcoming as defined and not as we would wish it defined.

Let us now reformulate the dilemma as follows:

> 'What might the leader do in this situation to meet the external requirement while maintaining a coherent educational mission for the school?'

Simply to suggest a course of action in which neat chains of cause and effect magically produce a 'better' school would be a travesty. There are many ways into this case study. If set as a test question to a range of experienced, successful headteachers it would produce a range of approaches, each bearing the stamp of an individual approach to change and each coloured by the values of that headteacher. Let us therefore look at the dimensions of the dilemma, rather than the elusive easy option.

Consensus on goals

The given strengths and weaknesses mentioned a clarity of mission alongside some of the criticized items. As the first chapter in this book emphasized, however coherent the mission, it needs translating into practices and processes if it is not to remain at the level of rhetoric. City High School may well need to embark on a planning cycle where goals and outcomes are discussed openly and in practical terms rather than as vague aspirations. As a school leader in this situation what practical steps would you take? The commentary above indicated some of the possible rationalizations which might be brought to bear on a leader's attempts to redefine school goals. If your first step is to convene some kind of post-mortem following the critical report, how would you handle it? Would you simply listen? Would you start with your own gloss on what has been said and written about the school? Some leaders might think it prudent to ask teachers some leading questions in these circumstances. You would want to know, for example, a) what they think the main messages of the audit are and, b) what actions should flow from those messages.

However painful it may be, you have no option but to involve staff in some such dialogue. Simply to say, 'This is the problem and here is the solution' will not do. What you want out of this exercise is a consensus on what should now happen, not another debate about what has already happened. In fact you may feel that you can even insist that every teacher give his or her opinion about where the school should now be going. In a mature professional community it is not really an option to have *no* opinion on such a fundamental matter.

Reinforcing strengths

Schools are rarely condemned *in toto* by external reports. This dilemma carefully offered a range of strengths at City High School. One danger of the inevitable soul-searching which accompanies external criticism is that good practice is impoverished by a concentration on the need for change in other areas. As a school leader in this situation, you are already engaged in a high-risk enterprise, ie, leading change to meet targets for improvement. You do not want to lose the quality of your pastoral support on the way or to risk those other areas of strength which have led to your stable pattern of recruitment.

Dealing with people

If this were real, and if you were the school leader concerned, you would be under considerable personal pressure. Imagine some of the following:

- Leading meetings where your own leadership is implicitly criticized.
- Having to insist that such and such a target is non-negotiable and vital to the future of the school, even in the face of rational and deeply-felt reasoning to the contrary.
- Asking your team leaders to take their teams in new directions and to adopt major changes in curriculum, pedagogy and assessment within constricted time scales.
- Telling some of your team leaders that they must rethink their leadership of their teams, build more common purpose, insist on more common practice and so forth.

Ask yourself what skills you would need in handling these challenges.

Summary

City High School's problems look serious. They would be tackled more easily by a newly appointed leader than by one in post already. Whatever approach you personally might adopt, you have to define the problems at an early stage. Your definition must start at the broadest level. You would not, for example, seize on a matter of detail such as homework policy and work out from that. You need to envisage a hierarchy or pyramid where the apex of the scenario is the desired future state of the school. The next level of the hierarchy is the themes for improvement *and* continuity. The lowest level of the pyramid is the detailed policies and practices which serve the higher levels. The higher you move up that pyramid, the stronger your own input must be. The lower levels of the pyramid can be infinitely mutable or negotiable provided that the whole thing still hangs together.

A quality problem

John has been teaching in your school for 15 years. Prior to that he spent four years in another local school. He is the longest-serving member of the English department and has a responsibility allowance which effectively makes him the assistant team leader. In fact, the allowance was given many years ago for a responsibility which is long since defunct. John is popular with the other four team members and with the staff generally. He sees himself as an experienced, competent and knowledgeable teacher. He has never had any particular problems of discipline or classroom management and students appear to respect and even to like him. He makes a fulsome contribution to sporting, cultural and other extra-curricular activities in the school. Against this background of solid professional experience, and indeed success, the following emerges over the course of a school year.

The headteacher receives three separate letters from parents of pupils in John's classes. Each is a reasoned, polite but insistent complaint concerning the quality of learning in those classes. Typical remarks include:

> 'Susan does receive regular homework but it is often trivial, undemanding and inappropriate.'
>
> 'Carl does not seem to be learning much at all in English. His grades are lower than for any other subject.'
>
> 'I talked to some other parents at the open evening and we were all concerned about the English teaching.'

The head of department and the headteacher discuss these letters with John. He has a plausible explanation for every point raised. He talks about unrealistic parental expectations, increasingly demotivated students and lack of parental awareness about new directions in the English curriculum.

Other members of the English team begin to mention problems associated with John. These include inattention to departmental business, unwillingness to contribute to curriculum development tasks and lack of awareness on his part of the implications of new curricula and assessment.

An internal school audit of pupil achievement across the curriculum unwittingly demonstrates that John's students perform significantly worse than comparable students in other groups in most cases.

Towards the end of the year a number of parents write asking that their children not be placed in John's classes next year.

Viewing the problem

Before getting caught up in the detail of this hypothetical but surely believable scenario, let us look again at some of the apparently objective information above. In reviewing that information some additional messages will emerge which will affect the leadership perspective on John's problem.

Parents' letters – what weight do you place on these? How would you know, for example, how the remaining majority of parents felt?
Message: check the information and cross-check it.

John's response – how do you weight this? Is he not correct in pointing to a range of factors affecting pupil motivation and achievement?
Message: there is a measure of 'relativism' in most issues of quality in teaching and learning. Be clear what the school's expectation is and beware of absolute measures.

Colleagues commenting – is it not acceptable for teachers to undergo cycles of higher and lower motivation and commitment to the job? Do you expect all staff to be constantly at the peak of performance and discretionary effort?
Message: your approach to John is not stimulated by random or unrepresentative criticisms. You are considering the *whole* contribution which he makes to teaching and learning with his classes over time.

Pupil outcomes – this looks like bad news but surely one teacher on a team has to be the 'worst' according to whatever indicator you are using, whether it is attendance, grades, incidences of bad behaviour reported, etc.
Message: by definition, 49 per cent of us are below average in a whole range of human activity. The issue here is not whether John is the 'worst', but whether his contribution is acceptable or not.

Parental requests – how far should these be heeded? Would you let parents, for example, choose teachers for their children? Presumably not.
Message: there are limits to parental influence in such matters but beware of the professional closing-of-ranks which so infuriates parents. Parents who take the trouble to formulate a well-reasoned and courteous criticism deserve to know that you have recognized a problem, even if you will disagree about a solution.

Reformulating the dilemma

Assume that there are no particular personal or medical circumstances affecting John's performance of his job. Most school leaders faced with this combination of circumstances would view the problem reasonably sympathetically. They would of course be at pains to reassure parents, to support the team leader with any interventions he or she may make and above all to assure John of their support in addressing the concerns raised. They would also, presumably, attempt to clarify points of detail in ambiguous allegations; for example, what does 'trivial homework' mean?

Our conventions of professionality suggest that in the end John would be asked to address the problem himself. Realistically, no school is going to invest massive staff development resources in order to tackle an issue of this order. Equally, no leader in this situation is going to bring to bear a massive array of legalistic devices on a teacher who is underperforming rather than incompetent.

Nevertheless, what is at stake here is no less than the *quality of children's learning*, and it is here that any sane formulation of this problem must begin.

A range of approaches

Underperforming colleagues pose your most challenging leadership tasks. A textbook approach would suggest:

- define the problem with John
- agree development needs
- set goals and targets
- provide good pastoral support
- review progress regularly.

Different school leaders might weight the 'support' and the 'goal setting' differently. Many would separate the two so that one senior colleague is supporting while another is reviewing progress.

Good psychology here also reminds us to separate the personality from the problem. The convention would be to be hard on the problem but easy on the person.

How far to go in supporting John?

We can only go so far in pretending to 'resolve' this dilemma. Whatever the personal dimensions of it, the school leader has to have in mind a bottom line of one sort or another. What is the minimum progress which is acceptable? What is a maximum level of complaint and comment which you would tolerate before your strategy of support and development became sharper or even legalistic? Are there limits to the time of senior colleagues which you will devote to John? It is all too easy in a professional environment, and especially in small schools, effectively to collude with underperformance by ignoring it or by taking such a low-key approach to it that nothing is ever improved. It is in such dilemmas that your true loyalties as a school leader are under their closest stress. Does the rhetoric of our commitment to the highest quality of children's learning survive the reality of human frailty?

Summary

Professionally staffed organizations will always have 'Johns'. Whatever we achieve in terms of collegiality and a healthy team spirit in schools there will always be colleagues who are on the margins of acceptable performance in post. As a leader you are now increasingly accessing the kind of statistical information which emphasizes John's problems. In particular, the performance of his students compared with those in other classes will now be more obvious to you than it would have been to previous generations of school leaders. In dealing with John, your best ally is a clear set of expectations which apply to *all* the teachers in the school rather than an arbitrary set of criteria erected for John's purposes. You will never be able to answer satisfactorily absolute questions such as 'Is he or she a competent teacher?' You should be able to determine whether he or she meets the expectations for competent teaching in *your* school at *this* time.

What to invest in?

One of the most significant large-scale changes in education policy in most Western systems in recent years has been the move to local financial management in schools. Variously called local budgeting, devolved financial management and, in the UK, Local Management of Schools (LMS), this movement for change is only now beginning to make a real impact on the way school leaders view their role and on the decisions they make.

LMS poses a number of dilemmas, not least of which is the insecurity, for many schools, of a budget driven by pupil numbers. Despite the many insecurities aroused by LMS, most school leaders have welcomed it, at least cautiously, because of the various potential freedoms which accompany the insecurity. The most significant of these freedoms is the capacity to target resources, within certain constraints, on priorities determined by the school rather than by outside bodies. At its simplest, a modern school receives a sum of money at the beginning of the financial year (or, more likely, in instalments). That sum, largely determined by a best guess at pupil numbers, has to be used to meet the school's legal obligations towards its pupils and their parents. Beyond tradition, precedent and certain logical constraints, there are few legal fetters on *how* that sum is to be used to meet those purposes. Thus, we now have areas of choice in school leadership which, though limited in practical terms, are nevertheless significant when compared with a decade ago.

How much choice?

The larger the school, the larger the budget; the larger the budget, the wider the choice. That much is logical. The practical constraints which limit how a budget is spent consist of:

- A minimum need to heat and light the school, to keep it clean and safe and in a sound condition.

- An expectation that the conventional accoutrements of a learning environment will be provided, ie, books, equipment, tables, chairs, specialist accommodation, relevant information technology, etc.
- An assumption that the school will employ an appropriately qualified group of teachers in sufficient numbers to meet its curriculum needs, including any special learning needs of particular categories of pupils.
- The necessity for employing types of staff other than teachers so that the school can run efficiently and effectively.
- A need to hold a small but permanent contingency fund against emergencies over and above any formal insurances which a school may take out.

So far this does not look like a lot of scope for choice! The rhetoric of local management envisages a school (its leaders and its governors) making plans for the spending of their budget so that the best possible learning outcomes can accrue.

However, in most British schools, the staffing budget alone, teaching and non-teaching, takes over 90 per cent of the total budget and much of the rest looks to be effectively mortgaged to no-choice areas such as energy, maintenance, cleaning, insurance and minimal equipment.

In fact, much of the apparent absence of real-choice in LMS is based on our tendency to plan incrementally. Politicians may find it attractive to envisage a school starting anew every year with the question, 'How can we spend this budget to promote learning in our school?' School leaders start from the reality of existing commitments, staff employed and parental expectations of continuity. In an uncertain economic climate they may also be starting out with a need to *reduce* overall expenditure. So, where is the choice?

Formulating the dilemma

The starting point for this dilemma is the word 'incremental'. School leaders all over the world have welcomed the principle of choice, but have been quick to point out how little freedom of movement there is in practice with local management. This is understandable and essentially true if you plan incrementally. If your spending assumptions are based on what you are already spending then your room for manoeuvre is restricted.

Rethinking incrementalism

Go back over the main expenditure headings in your school. Heretical though this will seem, try this exercise. Start with the one-line budget and sketch out how you would ideally spend that budget in order to deliver your commitments to your clients. Do not be constrained by precedent. If you did this exercise, even perhaps as a training exercise with colleagues, you would doubtless come up with ideas which contradicted certain existing spending patterns. If the exercise looked too daunting, then try this simple knee-jerk reflection:

> An anonymous benefactor has promised the school a one-off donation equivalent to 5 per cent of its total annual budget. The only proviso to this donation is that it be used to improve the quality of learning in the school. How would you spend the money?

Whatever you answer to this question, one quick riposte would be, 'If you could guarantee improvement to children's learning by spending such a small percentage of your budget on that, then why are you not already planning to do that next year?'

The serious message underpinning these intellectual exercises is of course that to take a radical view of choice you have to discard a lot of assumptions about how we match resources to learning needs. Whatever your own view is, we can suggest with some certainty that a) we have a very imperfect knowledge of how a concrete process such as spending money produces an elusive outcome such as children learning and b) whatever that relationship between money and learning, there is a powerful intermediary called a teacher who is necessary to the transaction and who does not come cheap!

Choice and teacher-costs

Far and away the biggest item in any school's budget is teacher costs. It is virtually impossible to reduce the 'cost' of any individual teacher, even if this were desirable. Nevertheless, teacher costs do vary. Permanently employed staff on promoted scales are more expensive than temporarily employed staff on basic salaries. Even to begin this discussion affronts many deeply-held tenets of how schools should work, how teachers should be treated and how effective and well-motivated professional climates emerge. It is dangerous to start talking about 'fewer' or 'cheaper' teachers as the route to more real choice in school leadership. On the contrary, most school leaders would like to be able to employ more and better-paid teachers and to continue to invest in their development. Nevertheless, heretical though it may be, we have to follow the analysis through even if we baulk at its implications.

Fewer and better? More and different?

In the early days of coming to terms with local management, one school leader grappling with the implications of choice and teacher costs said at a seminar, 'I could run my school very effectively with 10 per cent less teachers if they were all as effective as the best of them – and I could give every one of them more money and still have change for other needs!' Such sentiments are of course unsurprising in a private professional discussion. That school leader may have been more cautious if the question of staffing costs had been raised formally in budget planning. The nub of the observation is nevertheless worth pursuing. Staffing ratios in schools are always a contentious issue, not least through proper concern on the part of teachers' associations for the working conditions of members. The number of individual teachers employed, whatever their contracts and conditions, will also be constrained by the need to provide specialist subject support. It is the case, however, that pupil-teacher ratios in similar kinds of school vary enormously, not only around the world but even between neighbouring schools in the UK which happen to fall on either side of an existing or previous authority boundary. There is no sacrosanct number of pupils per class above which learning cannot occur. What are the implications, then, of the fewer-teachers-better-paid strategy?

- Those teachers would have to teach more hours in the week or bigger classes, or a combination of the two.
- With their additional workload, they would have less discretionary effort available for other contributions to the life and work of the school.
- They might require a trade-off in terms of administrative or technical support: 'I'll happily do more of what I'm good at and paid for if you provide help with my xeroxing, record keeping and resource management.'

Despite these provisos, you might still think that in the end, the school's needs would be well served by such an option. The trouble with such imaginative thinking is not only the assumptions it overturns, with all the attendant risks and challenges, but the even more radical scenarios which suggest themselves as a result of that thinking. If you unfreeze assumptions about staffing in one dimension, you then question other dimensions. Take the traditional model of Teacher + 30 pupils + classroom = starting point for learning. If you concede that this can, if the circumstances are right, become teacher + 35 then why not the following:

(TEACHER x 2) + (2 x LEARNING ASSISTANT) + 100 PUPILS

Many primary schools already make extensive and imaginative use of paid adults other than qualified teachers in delivering their curriculum. As ever, there is a trade-off in such arrangements. Parental expectations of class size and the availability of individual attention for their child are a powerful brake on experimentation. Any such departures must be properly explained and justified to those parents.

Choice and technology

The current and likely future state of educational technology, particularly information systems and their rapidly falling costs, make some even more radical scenarios conceivable. The failure of learning machines in the 1960s may well prove to have been a failure of technology rather than a failure of principle. Even in the resource-limited context of the 1990s we can conceive of a near future in which the notion of every child in the school having an electronic work station is believable. The rapid take-up of CD-ROM and other technologies demonstrates how attractive such ideas can be, even in schools totally committed to small classes. In fact, even if schools do nothing to move towards this future, events are likely to overtake them. Availability of cheap pocket computing coupled with advances in telecommunications suggest that pupils may eventually equip themselves with technology enabling them to access limitless information. It is easy to forget that in the early 1970s some schools considered banning calculators because they enabled pupils to bypass certain mathematical processes!

Talk now – choose later

As a school leader how do you view all this? With horror? With interest? None of these changes can fail to affect our traditional assumptions about where to deploy resources to enable children's learning. One description offered of the teacher's place in this changing context was that of the teacher as a manager of learning, rather than a deliverer of it. No one seriously doubts that schools will continue to employ qualified teachers – and probably in numbers comparable to current levels – for a long time yet. Nevertheless, the school leader who is alive to these areas of choice will already be initiating discussions about the future of the learning transaction in his or her school.

Summary

The dilemma of choice in allocating the scarce resources in your school will grow rather than diminish in the foreseeable future. You will be under enormous pressure from teachers and parents to choose conservatively. In planning for the future, however, you cannot plan to replicate the past. As the choices proliferate, and particularly if you are in the fortunate position of planning for an increased resource base, do not forget what those choices are about: how best to spend money in order to produce learning outcomes for your clients. With this in mind, you may make some quite radical choices provided that you can justify them in terms of the quality of teaching and learning. The leader in these dilemmas must think ahead of the other partners; he or she must explore the different scenarios and insist that they are fully debated and evaluated. Successful school leaders do this; in thinking the unthinkable they enable change to occur dynamically and productively. The alternative is to allow the school to drift along with patterns of unchanging teaching and learning until change is forced through outside pressure.

Difficult people

This section consists of a sample of difficult interpersonal problems which school leaders typically confront. The samples are accompanied by commentary on the leadership challenges raised along with practical suggestions for dealing with them.

A source of stress

Responses from school leaders when asked what they find most challenging or difficult in their jobs suggest that it is the apparently intractable interpersonal problems which distress them most of all. Experienced leaders seem able to cope with remarkable degrees of change. They embrace complex new concepts with ease, they master new skill and competence areas, they face financial problems with equanimity and they shrug philosophically in the face of political perfidy. Yet, get them on to the subject of their difficult colleagues and they visibly collapse. Reason flies out of the window, logic is impossible and hope dies. It is these close-to-home problems which cause stress and sleepless nights, not the big-picture issues. No one who has worked in a complex organization will be surprised at this. In schools especially, the degree of mutual trust and respect necessary for the organization to function effectively is considerable. It is difficult to imagine any organization where the basic business can be so easily subverted or disrupted without anyone breaking their contracts or acting illegally. Merely to withhold goodwill and cooperation can destroy the learning environment in a school.

Leaders are also difficult people

Conversely, of course, school leaders themselves are a powerful potential source of stress, frustration and angst to those who look to them for leadership. It is axiomatic that if people in organizations are asked about barriers to their doing a good job, or reasons for frustration in their job, they invariably point to the attitude, actions or personality of someone at a different (usually higher) level of authority. Thus, gatherings of deputy headteachers or vice-principals can produce rich and often virulent unsolicited testimony to the shortcomings of their heads and principals. Middle managers in large schools vent many of their own frustrations on the perfidy of senior managers in general and junior staff are prone to view their own progress, or lack of it, through the filter of their team leader's behaviour. All of this will be familiar enough to any amateur student of organizational behaviour and indeed the funnier side of it is the raw material for much comedy in the arts generally.

The cost of difficult people

What we should not lose sight of, however, is the serious implication for organizational health and effectiveness where problems between professionals start to impinge on organizational life. If you are spending a lot of time on these kinds of problems this is time not spent on the core mission; thus the opportunity cost is considerable. Furthermore, there is the hidden cost of diverting energies away from other colleagues because of these dilemmas. Just as teachers worry about spending 50 per cent of their time on two pupils in a class of 30, so you should worry if the majority of teachers get little or no support from you because you are taken up with the one difficult colleague.

Interestingly enough, relatively few of these sources of frustration on the part of school leaders relate to incompetent or underperforming teachers. As you will see, the problems are more subtle and are not susceptible to easy solutions.

Case A: 'My blighted career'

Typically, this concerns a long-serving teacher in the school who sees herself passed over for promotion as younger teachers gain posts of responsibility ahead of her. Over time, she begins to feel that the school leader has something against her which he will not articulate. She repeatedly asks why she did not get such and such a job. She is repeatedly told that the job went to the best applicant and that this is no reflection on her competence or potential. She becomes embittered and, too late, makes a rash of applications for unsuitable senior posts elsewhere. Her failure in these applications merely increases her bitterness. She now sees the leader preventing her advancement elsewhere, having thwarted her on home territory.

Case B: 'I get on perfectly well with people'

Typically, this dilemma concerns a teacher who has poor interpersonal skills with colleagues but does not recognize the fact. He is a source of major frustration to colleagues in meetings, in daily communication and with parents. He is a poor listener. He is (unconsciously) rude in interrupting colleagues and in speaking *at* parents rather than talking with them. No one wants him on their team because he is the nemesis of good professional dialogue. The school leader, invariably, grasps the nettle at some stage and spells out some of these issues and problems to the teacher in words of one syllable. He listens, but does not hear. He refutes the criticism, reminding the leader that professional tittle-tattle and prickly sensibilities are one thing, but being an effective teacher is another – and no one doubts his teaching prowess!

Case C: 'I can't understand why anyone else has trouble with them'

Some schools have very demanding and challenging pupils. In such schools, the best of teacher cultures is that of shared approaches, mutual support and constant encouragement. The worst of cultures is that of the rugged survivalist.

Typically in this dilemma, the teacher has excellent control in the classroom through a combination of fine teaching skills, personal charisma and stern discipline. She achieves outstanding pupil outcomes and, to parents and others outside the school, is a paragon of what teachers should be and do. Inside the school, she is a constant source of resentment to colleagues who struggle to stay afloat in this difficult school. She simply cannot see why other teachers do not follow her example. She sees their problems in a simplified light – 'they are not trying hard enough' – and is not shy of repeating this to anyone who will listen.

Case D: 'I've only got seven years to go'

Ageism of any sort is the curse of professional environments. The notion that people are too young to lead at 30 and too old at 50 is a logical nonsense. Our emphasis on age is partly explained by the peculiar age distributions in the teaching profession. Since entry to the profession is largely demand-led it is hardly surprising that various baby booms mean a preponderance of teachers clustered around the 50 mark by the end of the century with relatively few 35–45 year-olds. Our culture also, in encouraging professionals to plan for and 'own' their retirement, has created a climate in which the final years of many careers are conducted with more than half an eye on the 'golden years'. It is hardly surprising then that proximity to potential retirement is used as an excuse note in so many circumstances. Typically this dilemma revolves around a senior member of staff, often a deputy, who is gradually extricating himself from strategic planning and leadership tasks and retreating into comfortable administrative concerns. School leaders who have described similar stories are usually very respectful of that deputy's abilities, virtues and achievements. What they find frustrating is the retreat from challenge under the guise of allowing a younger generation to take on important tasks of leadership. What they find difficult is to re-energize that colleague without patronizing them.

Case E: 'Don't trust them an inch'

Schools are not always the consensual, collegiate environments we would like them to be. Statistically, there will be teachers in any group who are, quite simply, not very nice people. This of course applies equally to school leaders, only since they are less numerous than other teachers, they are less noticeable! Professional organizations are of course hedged about with conventions and assumptions which make straightforward bad behaviour both rare and difficult to sustain. Teachers tend not to run amok, strike each other or swear at colleagues. The kind of case mentioned frequently in this context by school leaders is an altogether more subtle problem.

Typically, it concerns a teacher who undermines the authority of the school leader by criticism, rumour and half-truth, always in informal contexts such as staff-room gossip. Such a person is concerned to distance senior staff from other junior colleagues. They may or may not articulate opposition to the leader's policies and practices in public debate. They are quick, however, to supply colleagues over coffee with the 'real' reason why something has been said, done or proposed. It is futile to speculate here *why* people do this. The impact of such behaviour ranges from the trivial to the seriously damaging. A word of caution, however. There is a thin dividing line between behaviour which is damaging to the organization and that which is a natural and healthy manifestation of the informal structure of that organization. Every school, even the smallest, has its informal structure of rumour, gossip, influence and even power. There are great dangers in attempting to interfere with or to control this informal structure. It is a healthy safety valve for emotion, frustration and the exchange of information. Where the school leader will wish to act – whatever course is taken – is where the basic health and purposes of the school are at risk.

Difficult people and the school leader

This set of cases, though hypothetical in detail, is drawn from real examples at a level of principle. We could speculate endlessly about different approaches to each of them. Whatever difficult people you have to deal with as a school leader, they will no doubt be different again. So, what are the common threads here which can inform your general approach to interpersonal challenges in school leadership?

Courage

At the risk of beginning one of those interminable lists of the characteristics of successful leaders which litter the writing on organizations and management, we must stress first of all how vital the exercise of courage would be in tackling the cases above. It is formidably difficult to confront fellow professionals about shortcomings in their performance, their dealings with colleagues or their efficiency. One is lost in admiration for those who can do it with tact, sensitivity and human decency while retaining the rigour of their purpose. Courage, however, has to come from somewhere. We are not talking here about the blind charge for glory but the measured realization that the needs of the school outweigh the temporary pain of the difficult dialogue. Courageous school leaders are more likely to be made than born – they have developed an order of priority in which the quality of the school's mission predominates. Your courage therefore comes from establishing simple principles in all these cases. The most fundamental of these principles is to determine what is important about each case. Do not get caught up with the surface issues. In case C for example, the underlying issue for you as leader is not the sensibilities of the resentful colleagues, it is the issue of what counts as good practice in teaching and learning. Either our colleague, in this example, is operating *within* the school's vision of good practice or she is not. If she *is*, then one of your approaches may be to enable her to explain and share aspects of her practice with others. Oblige her to engage in positive dialogue about how she operates, why she does it that way and what benefits she aims for. Simply to ask her to tone down her comments or to say less about her successes is to avoid what is important in this dilemma.

In case A, the courageous leader will be clear – even to the point of embarassment – about why the colleague has not been promoted. You will also wish to find out whether she has serious aspirations to move elsewhere or not. If she has, then help with pointed advice about applications, interviews and the like. If she really does want to stay with you, do not arouse unrealistic expectations about her career in the school. What you have to do is retain that teacher's confidence and motivation. Being ambiguous with her about things which clearly matter to her will not achieve that.

Integrity

School leaders are rarely saintly figures! Nevertheless, their own personal integrity is not only under constant examination, it also powerfully sets a tone and an example by which others feel entitled to behave. This is not a time to mince words. If the leader misleads, mistreats or misrepresents his or her colleagues in any serious way, he or she forfeits trust, respect and, in extreme cases, collaboration. Any lapse of integrity needs atonement through word or deed. Admit mistakes, apologize for hurt and offence, explain bad decisions. Leadership is not a test of strength and teachers are immensely forgiving where frailty is conceded.

Empathy

Are you a good listener? This is not a facetious question. Just as the Light Brigade charged to tragedy on an ambiguous message, so many school leaders have misread interpersonal problems in schools through rusty antennae. Self-disclosure is hard enough for the average person, but the professional environment is doubly difficult since we are expected to be reasonably self-sufficient and self-motivating in our jobs. You may be instinctively empathetic with your teachers and with their problems but you may have difficulty in creating an atmosphere in which these can be discussed freely. It would not be useful advice simply to say 'be empathetic'! If you have a problem here, try delegating some of those more sensitive discussions to other senior colleagues. If you are unsure how your colleagues view your own interpersonal skills then you could do worse than ask them – and ask them to be brutal!

In case B, for example, any lack of empathy on your part will prevent you from making progress with that colleague. Presumably what you want in this dilemma is for the teacher concerned to see for himself that his behaviours are detrimental to effective teamwork and thus to the broader success of the school. You are trying to make him more of an extended professional, ie, someone who can see how good practice in planning and evaluating in teams links naturally with good practice in the individual classroom. This is a subtle challenge for you as leader. Remember that there will inevitably be times when your leadership intervention actually makes things worse rather than better. Delegation need not be abdication.

Persistence – up to a point!

Because dealing with difficult colleagues is in itself so difficult and draining, and because there are easy rationalizations available ('life's too short, it won't make any difference in the end', etc.) it is tempting to give such problems as those identified above one good shot only. It may be even more tempting, metaphorically, not even to get the gun out. Unlike more conventional organizational problems and dilemmas, those which turn on issues of personality, attitude and behaviour are worryingly open-ended. They seem to lend themselves less easily to rational strategies such as deadlines, targets and action plans. You are unlikely to put 'Must sort out Jeremy's personality clash with Sarah' on your to-do list for Monday morning since to do so would affront the logic of time management.

To return to where we started with difficult people, you should not minimize the long-term damage to the school from interpersonal problems being allowed to linger and fester. The reason why so many school leaders lose sleep over such issues is not just that they are difficult to resolve, or personally painful to confront, it is also because of the diversion of time, energy and goodwill from the main purposes of the school. This is why you need to act, why you should set limits to your action and why you should, in certain cases, insist on some kind of resolution to the problem. This means having deadlines, where appropriate, spending – but limiting – your own quality time on the issue, and being clear to individuals where, in your judgement, the well-being of the school's wider purposes are at risk.

For each of the cases identified, the following logic should operate:

1. What is fundamentally at stake (define)?
2. Is (what is at stake) important to the life of the school?
3. What outcome would best serve the school's interests?
4. Share that desired outcome with the parties concerned.
5. Establish time scales within which progress will be acknowledged.
6. Be ruthless with yourself about who should be involved with what kinds of interventions. If you have doubts about your own sensitivity or empathy, then delegate – but delegate within the spirit of stages 1 to 4 above.

Problems and the leader

In this chapter we have considered a wide range of critical dilemmas. Inevitably there are massive gaps. No doubt you are currently preoccupied with a totally different set of challenges. Nevertheless, what surfaces through all of these examples and what characterizes a positive approach to the critical areas of leadership choice is a *will* to solve problems. Leaders are not paid to respect and avoid problems and dilemmas, they must address them. This may seem a rather lame point on which to end such a complex topic, but it is entirely apposite. You will be beset with problems as a school leader. You will, in the spirit of the age, wish to turn every problem into a challenge and you will spread optimism about the school's capacity for dealing with its problems. Through all this, you have to want to overcome difficulties. There are few sadder prospects in the world of education than the school leader colluding with the pessimism of the age. Don't go into the staff room and nod sagely at the 'isn't it all dreadful' chat. Remind colleagues every day why you are all there, what admirable things the school is achieving and what it can achieve in the future. Finally, smile a lot – it is another of the things you are paid to do!

Summary

The school leader is uniquely placed to define and interpret educational dilemmas and problems. Although the majority of these dilemmas will revolve around the three themes of 'quality', 'people' and 'choices', the underlying issue – and the best starting point for solutions – is how any dilemma relates to the basic mission and purpose of the school. The courage and integrity required to confront organizational dilemmas is born of a clarity and objectivity about what the school is there for and what it is trying to achieve. Where dilemmas devolve on to apparently intractable problems of human relations, leaders need to set limits to the time and energy which will be applied to those problems before it is acknowledged that the wider health of the organization is at risk. Above all, the successful school leader will be orientated to solving problems and confronting dilemmas rather than to avoiding or respecting them.

Education is often an ambiguous business. Without leadership, ambiguities tend to multiply and expand. The firmness of your own approach to problems sets a tone within the school. It is not the case that successful leaders do not have problems, but it is the case that they have fewer problems. If teachers and others in the school's community perceive that the leader is prepared to seek solutions in the wider interests of the school then they are less likely to let ambiguities and minor problems develop into major dilemmas.

Chapter 5
Leadership and Accountability

This chapter combines the themes of accountability and evaluation in school leadership. It attempts to place current debates about educational accountability in context and to suggest a proper set of priorities for school leaders in considering their approach to evaluating the effectiveness of their schools.

Myths and demons of accountability

If you have followed an academic course in education in the last decade, or if you have ever listened to a learned discourse on 'Whither education?', you will be familiar with some or all of the following:

'Accountability started with the oil crisis in the early 1970s.'

'It is the same all over the world; Western societies have lost faith in mass education and are blaming the schools and the teachers for a range of social and economic problems.'

'Education is now subject to the same consumerist pressures as any other publicly available product.'

'We must all get used to a variety of demands for accountability from important audiences.'

'The secret garden of the curriculum has been opened up for scrutiny from outside.'

All these points revert to a conventional wisdom which is now firmly embedded in educational thought. That conventional wisdom suggests that in the late twentieth century, the public in general, and politicians in particular, somehow realized that education was not 'delivering the goods' and that schools should be made publicly accountable for a range of outcomes. Those outcomes should be easily understood and should relate to 'common sense' views of what counts as effective education. They are usually defined as scholastic attainment (in whatever form), attendance and related statistical information and measures of teacher performance.

This conventional wisdom reappears in education-speak in many guises, from learned commentaries on particular policy issues to casual teacher talk about what 'they' are doing to 'us'. It is a very dangerous and ultimately destructive conventional wisdom. It distracts attention from important questions of school improvement. It risks validating a range of negative approaches to change and it threatens to enmesh school leaders in a cycle of pessimism from which many may not emerge. Of course, governments who attempt to redefine the content, process and outcomes of something as sensitive as schooling take enormous risks. Where their policies have a populist flavour ('get back to basics', 'sack bad teachers', etc.) they inevitably invite conflict with the insiders, the educationalists who have to deliver reform and change. No professional can abide the thought that a specialist, finely-honed craft is being undervalued, traduced or otherwise redefined by lay amateurs. The temptation for school leaders to join these debates about accountability is enormous and the purpose of this chapter is not to persuade you to withdraw from public debate about important educational questions but to encourage you to re-think where true accountabilities lie so that when you try to answer the question, 'How are we doing?', you are answering it for the right audience, in the right manner and on the right territory.

Accountable for what? To whom? How?

Try this simple exercise. Write down a list of those bodies, interest groups or individuals to *whom* you feel accountable as a school leader. For each entry you have made, suggest *what* it is that you are accountable for to those persons or bodies. Finally, say *how* (ie, what is the actual mechanism by which) you are accountable. If you can do that exercise for any or all of the bodies or groups identified you should now take a long cool look at what you have written and consider this simple question: *'Does it work?'* The answer to that question is no doubt something like 'up to a point, Lord Copper' or some variation of the curate's egg metaphor. Simply doing such an exercise, even as a mental note, tells you that:

- the number of accountabilities is vast,
- the nature of those accountabilities (ie, accountable for what) is complex, and
- the mechanisms of accountability vary enormously in their effectiveness.

You may even have given up at the stage of 'accountable for what?' as you wrestled with words like 'standards', 'quality' and 'effectiveness' and despaired of ever obtaining a consensus on what those words mean in practice.

EXAMPLE

Accountable to whom? – Parents

I (we) are accountable to the parents of all the pupils in the school.

Accountable for what?

We are accountable to them for the care and custody of their children, for the provision of relevant and challenging curricula, for scholastic outcomes, for the provision of sporting and cultural opportunities, for meeting statutory obligations, for reporting on progress and so on *ad infinitum*.

What are the mechanisms of accountability?

The mechanisms are: termly reports, newsletters, publication of results, involvement in school governance, annual parents' meetings and access by parents to teachers in the school.

Does it work?

The annual meeting is effectively ignored, parents only visit when their own child has a problem, the newsletter is only read by a minority; no one stands for election to governors; they appreciate the reports but they don't understand the published results.

If your analysis was similar to this, do not despair! As ever, when trying to consider what is important in education and in evaluating how well those important things are being done, we risk ending up in a morass of conflicting values, pressures and needs. Let us therefore look at accountability from a fresh starting point.

Defensive accountability

Drawing up complex accountability webs or listing accountabilities can make for a very negative approach to leadership. Such exercises remind you more of your administrative, managerial and political responsibilities than your responsibilities as the leading educator in the school. There are many risks in moving from a state in which school leaders are still educationalists to one in which they are largely administrators and managers. Perhaps the most disturbing of these risks is the spectre of school leaders buried under paperwork, struggling with resource dilemmas and so fearful of the encircling net of accountability that they only ever lead reactively or defensively. No one wants this to happen. Anyone with a stake in the effectiveness of schools would want the school leader to be confident, pro-active and highly engaged with the real business of the school. What you need to do therefore is to distinguish between defensive and offensive accountability.

Defensive accountability, at its simplest, means having efficient and effective procedures in place for dealing with all those legal and conventional demands for information and reports which the school will face routinely. Offensive accountability is the territory where you *choose* to demonstrate success, worth and achievement. The difference between the two is not always easy to distinguish. Some leaders would, for example, treat much of what counts as accountability to parents as defensive while others would see it as offensive. No matter: for your own sanity as a leader and for the health of the school you have to make these distinctions so that your creative energy can go to the offensive side of the equation.

Defensive accountabilities will certainly include:

- legally required statistical information
- financial information
- regularly updated information summarizing curriculum and teaching arrangements
- statements of school policy

- procedures for reporting to parents
- any documentation likely to be required by local and national inspectors as part of their statutory interventions.

The list will go on and is formidable enough. However, what characterizes most of these items is that they are at least predictable. Effective leaders do not wait for such accountabilities to arise: they plan for them, they delegate appropriately for the gathering of information and they ensure prompt availability. With modern information management systems, much of the data required for routine accountability mechanisms are easily handled. Much of them are in any case common in that the same information about curriculum policy may be lifted and incorporated in a variety of different reports. Defensive accountabilities should not be played down or taken lightly. Many of them *do* require creativity and corporate energy. All of them are important. Most of them have an easy internal logic which helps you to fulfil them. As a leader you will give them a very high priority but they do not in themselves answer all the important questions about accountability which should engage you.

Accounting offensively

Christopher Price, a former education minister, addressing a headteacher audience in 1993 reminded his listeners of the strong radical tradition of school leaders in the UK. He also reminded his listeners that 'great' headteachers, like other 'great' leaders, have usually disdained conventional accountabilities. Of course this is dangerous talk and should not be taken as practical advice for school leaders! Nevertheless, his comments remind us, rightly, that school leaders who make a difference to the quality of schooling often go beyond conventional accountability. They choose their own ground on which to give an account of what the school is achieving and they choose their own methods for doing it. This is the essence of offensive accountability. It is the difference between fulfilling a legal requirement to publish some students' test scores and writing to a group of parents about the quality of work achieved by that group of students. It is the difference between publishing a required end-of-year financial statement and talking to parents about how specific investment of resources is being geared to specific learning outcomes. It is the difference between the school brochure which reassures potential parents that legal curriculum requirements are observed and the brochure which, in addition, trumpets the areas of excellence which the school is building as part of its own vision for the future.

Where to account offensively

All the major leadership concerns about accountability ultimately come down to issues of quality. Your consumers, your partners and your political overseers all want quality at the input, process and output stages of the educational transaction. Your own offensive accountability will recognize this and will start from those areas of the school's life and work where quality is at stake. Where you are setting out to give a good account of the school, therefore, you will concentrate your energies on core educational issues. At the risk of repetition, these issues will be those of teaching, learning and the care and support which enables them to happen. The care and support are interesting foci for your offensive accountability.

Throughout this book there has been a strong emphasis on the leader engaging with fundamentals of teaching and learning. A school which ignores or downplays its pastoral responsibilities to young people will not only be a sterile and unwelcoming environment for learning, it will also risk constant friction with parents who expect a high degree of care and control from schools as well as the 'shaping' effects of the pastoral curriculum. Most defensive accountabilities have little to say about care and support and even less about the pastoral curriculum. They are assumed to be there and to work effectively. In actively promoting your school, therefore, you should consider what is distinctive about the climate for pupils in it. Take the issue of bullying in schools, for example. What do we know about it? We know a lot – and not very much! We know that:

- it is widespread and under-reported
- it occurs in many different age groups and across genders
- it can destroy individual lives, maim psychologically and, in rare examples, lead to real tragedy
- it is as likely to be happening in a privileged private school as in an inner-city state school
- most teachers have knowledge of bullying from their own school days and, statistically, many teachers will have been bullied, and been bullies.

We do not know:

- precisely what makes bullies
- how much bullying there is
- how to stop it
- how to prevent it ever happening again

Worst of all, perhaps, we are unsure of how to deal with the issue as part of our information to parents and as part of our promotion of the school as a caring and supportive environment. You can be sure, however, that parents whose children are bullied will generally blame the school. Where bullying becomes a local media issue a school can suffer massive damage to its image. Equally, from the leader's perspective, to have a policy on bullying and an elaborate set of practices and procedures for dealing with it, can look like an admission that you have problem in your school! The offensive accountability is clear here: you must have a policy and you should treat this as a strength. For every parent who is uneasy about seeing the issue raised at all, there will be many more who will be relieved that bullying is recognized and that it is dealt with. Where you have put a lot of time and effort into addressing the issue, and where you are particularly proud of what you have achieved, why not publicize this?

What is your school known for?

Image and reputation in education are fragile flowers. We may despair of the modern emphasis on marketing, publicity and image in schools but we cannot ignore it. It is now conventional for schools to cultivate local media and to ensure a regular flow of news items reflecting credit on the school. Most schools now also make considerable efforts to ensure that publicity material, and particularly the school's brochure, is attractively presented.

Where a school's image is geared to competing for pupils with other local schools then these concerns become at the same time more important *and* more dangerous. They become more important because the reality of parental choice means that schools which lose out in such competition lose financially and, ultimately, may risk closure. They become more dangerous because unlike most other services and products, education as a service only has a fixed number of 'buyers', ie, those parents with reasonable access to your school who have children of entry age. Slick marketing, if practised by every school in the area, merely leads to a spiral in which increasing time, energy and money are devoted to simply maintaining a viable market share. There is already a dangerous preoccupation with marketing in many schools.

Get these questions of image and market in perspective. What, ultimately, will sell your school to prospective parents? Glossy brochures? A free stationery pack for all new pupils? (This has actually happened in England). A special deal on insurance policies for parents? (This also). No. For most schools most of the time, the level of pupil entry is determined by inertia factors rather than through the active exercise of parental choice. Most of your pupils are with you because you are the local school, because siblings attended the school, because peers and friends went there or, perhaps most prosaically of all, because you are the only school around. Choice *is* clearly exercised by a significant minority of parents who go to the effort of weighing up the relative merits of competing schools and who look for the best placement for their particular child. Yet even where choice is conscious, the impact of word-of-mouth, rumour, gossip and reputation will far outweigh anything the school can mount as a one-off exercise to market itself to prospective parents.

What is it then that informs rumour, gossip and word-of-mouth? Aside from the unusual or striking factors such as scandal, criminality, arson, tragedy or failure, reputation is largely determined by the experiences of the school's existing clients. Some policy issues such as whether the school requires uniform will always be contentious but these are not areas where you have a lot of latitude: either you have uniform or you do not and whatever the image a uniform projects, it is clearly the case that the uniform by itself means little. However, one parent who feels aggrieved by the school's treatment of her child will project an image of the school to her peer group which transcends any cosmetic question of uniform. By contrast, parents whose experience of the school is of an ordered, caring and purposeful environment in which their children learn and grow, are powerful ambassadors.

How can you capitalize on the positive experiences of your clients in order to promote an image of the school which reflects your core purposes?

Selling success

Do not assume that all your clients are as aware about your school's successes as you are. We are perhaps a little naive about our marketing in schools. We strive to have cultural, sporting and social events and successes reported in the local media. We are pleased if our school performs well in tests or examinations where outcomes are published and comparisons with other schools made. On the other hand, school leaders are frequently upset and angry when a single unfavourable mention or negative comment is made about their school. They feel that the single criticism is unfair or unrepresentative. They plead that this criticism ignores the excellent work being done every day and maligns the outstanding commitment of the vast majority of pupils and teachers.

You cannot blame local media for seizing on error, scandal or failure. By North American standards, the British media are in fact remarkably gentle in dealing with schools. The majority of mentions which your school receives will be not only favourable and literal but largely uncritical. They will publish the photograph of your winning football team and name each player in the caption. They will write up your charity concert and laud it for its energy and worth. However, the rare occurrence of a story which reflects badly on a school is in a different category of 'news' and, however good your relations with the local media, you cannot be surprised when they find real 'news' as opposed to regular, polite coverage. As a school leader you have to live with this but you *can* affect the overall balance of messages about your school which go to parents and others.

Dealing with the media

Make sure that where you are looking for media interest and coverage, that coverage is as much about important educational concerns as it is about sporting, cultural and social matters. Innovations in teaching and learning and in the use of educational resources can be as newsworthy – and much more powerful in shaping your image – as the lower-level coverage.

Active accountability to parents

First, keep in regular communication with parents about what the school is doing in its core mission. School leaders often complain that parents are reluctant attenders at events which publicize curricular and pedagogical matters. This is true. It is also the case that most school-to-home communication, other than formal reports to parents, is largely about anything *but* teaching and learning. You do not create a climate overnight in which parents regularly involve themselves in dialogue and other communication about teaching and learning. You have to start somewhere. Write to parents regularly about what is going on in the curriculum, in their child's class and with their individual child. If the first time you invite parents in to talk about teaching and learning only a fraction of the class or year group turn up, then write to the others with a summary of what happened and publicize the next event at the same time. Experiment with different formats for what counts as 'parents' evening' or 'open evening'. Vary your communication with parents. Don't rely on densely printed newsletter formats. Modern desktop publishing techniques enable you to produce attractive and imaginatively formatted documents cheaply. Involve the pupils in the design of these materials. You want to be in a position where every parent can, in theory, answer the 'What have you been doing in school recently?' question without even asking their child.

Second, demand feedback and use it to project the school. One principle which pervades all successful modern commercial organizations is the relentless pursuit of customer feedback. This is not a difficult principle to pursue in schools. Unlike organizations which are selling goods and services to an anonymous and unpredictable public, schools are dealing with a relatively small and easily accessed group of clients. For practical purposes these clients are parents, pupils and the local community. What steps can you take? Some of these suggestions will be familiar to you and you may be following them already, others may be less so.

Practical strategies

- Have a standard tear-off slip accompanying most of your communications to parents. The slip invites comment on any aspect of the school's service. One teacher takes responsibility for monitoring this information and producing regular summaries.
- Questionnaire surveys. What main policies for improvement are you following as a school this year? Construct a simple tick-box questionnaire around that policy and send it either selectively to parents in particular classes or to the whole parent group.

- Delegate evaluation tasks to pupil or parent groups. Older pupils in particular may make more successful enquiries or evaluations than teachers in sensitive areas such as attitudes to homework, aspects of discipline or other social issues.
- Invite community representatives to the school, not to lecture them on what a wonderful job you are doing but to listen to them and to learn what their perspective on the school is. How do they feel about the way pupils behave in the vicinity; how the premises are accessed by other user-groups; your regular fund-raising efforts?
- Reconsider, if you have not already done so, the format and 'feel' of those occasions where you are inviting parents into the school for consultations. What is the experience of these occasions for the parents? Waiting in queues to see teachers? Being talked at by senior staff? What do you want them to feel? Relaxed? Able to talk? Free to question and to give opinion? Always include on these occasions opportunities for parents to talk freely with teachers outside the pressures of the one-to-one 'my child' agenda or the intimidating arena of the mass meeting.
- Where you have sought feedback, especially where that feedback has been time-consuming for the participants, always try to get a summary of that information back to the people who supplied it originally. This need be no more than a note telling the parents in that class that the survey about homework revealed that the majority of parents and pupils are happy with current arrangements but that two parents raised important matters of repetition in tasks set and these have now been sorted out by the teachers concerned. One short paragraph, but a powerful signal to those parents that a) the school seeks feedback for a purpose, b) listens to it carefully, and c) does something about it. Those parents will then give a particular message to their peers and contacts in the community when your school is being discussed.

Making sense of feedback

There is an interesting comparison with the role of a travel agent in what schools are trying to do when they ask their clients about the quality of their services. As we well know in education, the pinning down of what precisely we are purveying is frustratingly complex and elusive. It is fraught with relativism and even when we have defined it we find it hard to evaluate it to the satisfaction of every conceivable audience. Travel agents, likewise, are purveying a complex and elusive notion called a 'holiday'. What is a holiday? It is largely an experience comprising a subset of other experiences. We will freely characterize a holiday as 'nice', 'superb', 'better than last year' or even 'terrible'. Of course, having spent money on a holiday you are psychologically inclined to deem it a successful experience even where there are flaws or frustrations. Travel agents have no compunction about evaluating this elusive and complex phenomenon. If they wish to remain in business they must maintain a high level of customer satisfaction leading to repeat business. Typically, then, they will ask you, either on a questionnaire or as part of an interview sample, a number of qualitative questions about your holiday. The key words in these questions will be 'like', 'happy', 'satisfied', 'adequate', 'sufficient', 'helpful', and of course the opposites of these words. Such questionnaires ignore the massive potential philosophical problems associated with the notion of 'Did you enjoy the food?'; they simply ask you whether you did or not. Without making an overly simplified comparison with a business which is vastly different from a school's business, there is nevertheless a reassuringly straightforward and applicable principle at stake here: how do you know how well you are doing if you don't ask the people involved?

A minimum task for any school leader interested in positive accountability should therefore be to ensure that all the school's clients have an opportunity at least once a year to answer simple questions about how well the school is performing in delivering its purposes.

Accountability and the governing body

One group vital to the governance of the school and inextricably linked with virtually all facets of the accountability web is the school governors. This is not the place to describe the detail of the legal and conventional mechanisms which surround the work of governors. Nevertheless, there are important dilemmas in the relationship between governors and school leaders which will affect the leader's approach to questions of accountability.

How do you view governors?

Here are some sample statements characterizing a range of possible attitudes to school governors on the part of school leaders:

- They are an unnecessary intrusion of lay influence in a professional world.
- They are a real manifestation of partnership in governance: without them, there would be no check on professional autonomy.
- They can never be expert enough about what is important in a school; they lack the ability to make educationally correct decisions.
- Governors are not tainted by insider definitions of the world: they represent the real consumers of education and are well placed to make decisions about what is important in a school.
- Governors have an intermittent and selective involvement with the school: school leaders have a permanent and total involvement, they can not walk away from problems.

Where do you stand in this debate? It would be foolish to pretend that individual orientation does not matter here. You are unlikely to cleave wholeheartedly to *any* of the sentiments above but some of them will more closely represent your personal view more than others. Within your own peer group of school leaders there are no doubt those whose attitude to their governors shocks you by its hostility and lack of respect. Equally you may have colleagues whose deference and submission to their governors you find just as difficult to swallow. You will certainly have experience or knowledge of conflict between governors and headteachers.

Leaders and governors – what kind of relationship?

We are still seeking what has been called an 'elegant' relationship between governors and senior staff in schools. Individual schools still demonstrate widely differing kinds of governor-teacher culture. Powerful personalities can still make a nonsense of convention or even of statute. The old caricature of a dyspeptic, bullying and capricious chair of governors riding roughshod over fellow governors and teachers alike has not disappeared entirely. Equally, the powerful headteacher cowing governors into submission and forcing their decisions through a puppet chair is also still to be found. Happily, most schools manage a relationship which if not elegant is at least moderately fit-for-purpose. Accountabilities are, in practice, rarely discussed and while this may not pose a problem for most of the time, an unclear or ambiguous accountability can return to haunt a school with unfortunate consequences.

Agreeing accountabilities

Some schools are blessed with virtually perfect governing bodies, well informed, efficient in their conduct of business, closely involved with the life of the school, sensitive, clear about the boundaries of power and responsibility and utterly dedicated to the success of the school. Some governing bodies are also blessed with perfect school leaders! In the absence of perfection – whatever that may be in this instance – the first practical steps that any school leader should take in establishing appropriate accountabilities is to discuss them. Despite a decade of major educational reform, large-scale change in the structure and functioning of governing bodies and a good availability of appropriate training, there is still a remarkable haziness in the minds of governors and school leaders alike about some of the boundaries of their respective roles and powers. If there were easy answers, of course, they would long ago have been written on one side of paper and committed to memory by those concerned! As a school leader, you need to be clear about a few fundamental aspects of these boundaries. This will then determine the kind of dialogue you initiate in order to get that clarity. So, what do you need to know?

- *Decisions*. Which kinds of decisions can you make without reference to governors and which should you refer?
- *Policy*. Which areas of policy will need governor involvement and which can be left to senior staff and teachers?
- *Information*. What are the information needs of the governing body, how are they to be met and by whom?
- *Involvement*. What is an appropriate level of involvement of governors in the day-to-day life of the school?
- *Staffing*. Which aspects of staff management are appropriate for governor involvement beyond legal aspects of recruitment, selection, discipline and dismissal?
- *Agendas and business*. How far do governors expect to set their own agenda items for governor business and what input will teachers, including yourself, make to it?
- *Inquiries, complaints and concerns*. What is the procedure for airing issues raised by parents and others via governors?
- *Quality and effectiveness*. How do governors expect school leaders to give a regular account for the quality of what the school is doing?

This is a formidable list, but can you really afford not to have a degree of clarity about these items in order to develop an appropriate climate of accountability?

It would be impossible to give here an ideal-type description which met each of these items. You might, however, imagine an acceptable range of approaches to dealing with each of them. The important thing for you is to clarify where your school stands within that acceptable range. There follows below a series of 'instances', each with commentary, to illustrate some of the eight items raised above. Each commentary suggests both acceptable and unacceptable approaches. You will doubtless disagree with some of the commentary, but that does not matter; the purpose of this commentary is to encourage you to undertake these clarifications with your own governors so that similar 'instances' can be dealt with against a backcloth of shared assumptions. Some similar instances have already been trialled as part of joint governor-senior staff training by the Oxford Centre for Education Management and the commentary reflects input from those training dialogues.

INSTANCE A

A governor visits the school as part of a pre-planned series of governors' visits. He spends time in one classroom where he observes the following phenomena:

- the class spends long periods copying material from a blackboard into exercise books
- two pupils finish tasks early and ask what they should do next. They are told to sit quietly until they are told what the whole class is doing next
- one pupil begins playing with a video game under the desk. The teacher strikes the child firmly but not violently with the back of his hand by way of rebuke. The pupil puts the game away and goes back to work.

Additional information: the governor is aware that the copying from the board is implicitly frowned on in the school's language policy. He is also aware that striking pupils is totally forbidden.

Commentary. Do not get caught up with the detail here. What is at stake is a principle of accountability. Whether the teacher is good/bad, right/wrong is not at issue. What should now happen and who should be involved?

Unacceptable approaches probably include: the governor saying and doing nothing, the governor raising it under 'any other business' at the next governors' meeting; the governor simply telling fellow governors and others informally about what he has seen.

Acceptable approaches probably include some combination of the following: the governor clarifying with the teacher what he has observed; the governor relating his experience to the headteacher and agreeing a course of action; the governor leaving action to the headteacher; the governor signalling informally to the head and chair of governors what has occurred and seeking guidance on how to involve governors in discussion of the issues raised. Put yourself in that headteacher's position. Without prejudicing the detail of any future dialogue with the teacher concerned, how do you view the accountabilities? What are your responsibilities now to that governor and to other governors? How can you deal with this while retaining a) the confidence and goodwill of teachers in welcoming governors, and b) the confidence of governors that their access to and involvement in the life of the school is not merely rhetorical but actually means something?

INSTANCE B

You have agreed a budget for the financial year with governors. As part of that agreement, governors insisted on conservative spending projections likely to lead to a surplus of a significant sum over and above normal contingency projections. Governors asked senior staff for a priority-ordered list of spending items to be activated in the likely event of that surplus being available. You devised and supplied such a list which contained three items. Nine months into the financial year, you reviewed the financial position with team leaders and budget-holders and foresaw not only the level of surplus which the conservative accounting had previewed but an unanticipated additional surplus from low energy costs in a mild winter. Your budget-holders rejoice and flourish endless lists of items which they desperately need, from books to computer hardware to specialist staffing support. The original list of three items agreed by governors now looks out-of-date and of a lesser importance than the new demands raised. You allow your budget-holders to exploit that surplus to meet their urgent needs. The next governors' meeting comes around and the financial report from you reveals the actual surplus. A governor asks when the list of three items will be activated and you explain what has actually happened.

Commentary This not simply a matter of 'Why didn't you tell the governors what was happening?' It is a clash of accountabilities and priorities. From a governors' perspective, they have carefully budgeted for a surplus and taken pains to ensure that the surplus is put to uses which the practitioners have determined. Why did the teachers change their minds? Can they not plan ahead? Have they no long-term vision of how resources can be best deployed to meet the learning needs of pupils? Why do we bother with all this patient consultation if the professionals are going to be this capricious? From the school leader's perspective, this simply illustrates the difference between those with an intermittent involvement with the school and those with a close and permanent involvement. Priorities change, new demands arise, needs foreseen evaporate with circumstances.

Unacceptable approaches probably include censuring the senior staff formally for their decisions, demanding spending oversight of every item above a certain value, and simply recognizing what has happened and ignoring it.

Acceptable approaches probably include the governors asking for a detailed rationale for the 'new' spending items, a reminder to the staff that expenditure priorities are governors' responsibility, however much is delegated, and a review of how priorities are established in a new financial year.

How do you view these accountabilities? You want to be certain that there is enough logic and predictability in your own planning so that conflict can be avoided. Do you actually accept that governors have real rights in determining how resources are deployed?

INSTANCE C

A group of governors is taking a particular view of quality issues in your school. While accepting that the school has admirable purposes, well-qualified and hard-working staff and a preponderance of pupils from impoverished socio-economic backgrounds, they are pushing senior staff to improve the hard measures of accountability in stark, instrumental ways. They want more regular testing in basic subjects, publication to governors of these results by pupil and by class so that internal comparisons can be made, harsher approaches to discipline and uniform and a stricter approach to grouping pupils by ability across and within classes. These governors between them represent a cross-section of parent, community and political interests. They have a simple and difficult to refute rationale: 'We are here as guardians of the health of the school, we are aware of what external audiences want of schools, we know that the outcomes we desire are attainable because other schools do it, we are accountable for quality and you (the school leader) are accountable to us'.

Commentary These governors have taken public rhetoric about quality, standards and governor power at face value and they wish to push the boundary of governor/teacher relationships to its limit. Can you separate the 'educational' issues involved from questions of accountability? At what point, assuming that you and your teacher colleagues are currently committed to rather different policies, does this become a real conflict or indeed a resigning issue?

Unacceptable approaches probably include simply reasserting existing policy and practice, trying to avoid the issues by pretending that the separation of powers leaves all these questions to the 'insiders' or forcing a vote of confidence in existing arrangements.

Acceptable approaches may include review and reformulation of curriculum and assessment priorities as a *joint* governor/teacher exercise. You might consider inviting those governors to meet with teachers and to explain and debate their position. You would certainly want to make available information, data, evaluations and statistics which support your current policies.

How do you view the accountabilities here? Is the school leader a neutral broker between competing power bases? Of course not. The leader is first and foremost an educationalist. Whatever change emerges from such crises or conflicts, it is those inside the school who have to carry out the daily tasks of teaching and of managing learning. Therefore your concern will be for what is possible and feasible as well as what is desirable. You will be endlessly patient in discussion, in furnishing and reviewing information and considering proposals. You will no doubt search your conscience to ensure that you are not simply defending an outdated *status quo*. You will do all these things but at some point you will turn around and firmly state your position about what is both desirable and feasible. Governors should not ask school leaders to embark on changes and directions where the leader cannot be sure that teachers will follow.

Governors rightly expect that school leaders will be accountable for the highest quality of school outcomes. They expect trust, reliability and efficiency. Ultimately, however, they must accept limits to the partnership where it concerns fundamental matters of teaching and learning. Governors should expect teachers to review and to be critical about curriculum and pedagogy. They should feel entitled to ask and to have answered any number of difficult questions. They can not, however, expect to determine change of the scale envisaged in the instance above where the professionals concerned deem it dangerous or impossible.

Before leaving the discussion, whatever your own position may have been on the accountabilities referred to, try to imagine the mirror image of the example given. Think of those governors as trying to *liberalize* the school: imagine them demanding an end to regular testing, a complete mixed-ability model of organization and a loosening of disciplinary codes. Would your attitude to the case study have been different?

Accountability and quality

Much of this discussion of accountability has been about practical concerns, about relationships and about the pressures of leadership in a complex environment. It is appropriate to round off the topic with an examination of the single word which pervades much of our agenda in school leadership, a word which reoccurs constantly in educational debate and yet another example of words used in educational discussion which risk losing any real meaning through constant abuse. The word is 'quality'.

If you have any heroines or heroes in your personal pantheon of school leadership, you can no doubt point to what their approach to quality was. A concern for quality is not new; one of the curses of much writing on organizations and leadership is the assumption that only now have we discovered some nugget of truth previously ignored by generations of sages, researchers and practitioners. Even the apparently modern rhetoric of 'total quality', 'zero-defect' and 'quality assurance' is distinctly middle-aged in its origins and its fundamentals would not have been so surprising to the early practitioners of scientific management a hundred years ago.

Nevertheless, the notion of quality is a useful and relevant filter for the school leader coming to terms with his or her accountabilities both inside and outside the school. If there are very few hard truths about educational outcomes, there are certainly enough aspirations to guide individual school leaders. You may wish to avoid the technical rhetoric of total quality management in your leadership of the school but some of its building blocks will enable you to view some of your leadership concerns in a sharper focus. Take the notion of 'zero defect', for example.

Zero-defect in a school?

As the term suggests, zero-defect implies a product, a process or a service which is to all intents and purposes perfect. In other words, it meets its specification. The zero-defect notion sits easily in a context where the very notion of a defect is clear and unambiguous. The door falls off a new car. A fountain pen leaks. Where the notion is applied to a service, rather than a hard product, the defect can be defined in terms of customer satisfaction, or indeed of customer perspective on satisfaction as in the example of travel agent evaluations in this chapter. Because both product and customer are such problematic concepts in educational organizations, we have been on the whole shy of applying any version of the zero-defect approach. After all, what would count as zero-defect in meeting every expectation that parents have of the education of their child in your school? However, this rationalizing evades the issue. We may indeed have problems defining excellence in much of what schools are concerned with but in pursuing our concerns in schools we do have a large number of processes and practices where a sense of defect is not only applicable, but also desirable. Some examples are given below.

Pupil attendance

Of course you are concerned with attendance and you diligently follow-up unexplained absences in your school. You are very conscious of public concern about truancy and you know that statistical information about attendance is often taken as an indicator of school quality by outside audiences. Nevertheless, whatever the current level of unexplained pupil absence, however trivial statistically and however rationalized, that is the defect level which you tolerate. What defect level will you tolerate next term, next year? Can you envisage a target of zero-defect? How would you achieve such a target? Would the necessary expenditure of time, effort and other resources be worth it?

Assessment of pupils' work

What is the quality standard for returning pupils' work to them? Is this left to individual teacher conscience? Is there an assumption of, say, a one-week delay? Three school days? Does it matter? If it matters, and if it isn't happening, would you consider agreeing a quality standard with teachers? Would you police this standard with spot checks? Perhaps not. This might be considered too intrusive on individual teachers. Nevertheless, it is hard for a school leader to even raise an issue of late return of pupils' work where *no* standard has even been discussed.

Conduct of meetings

Do all meetings have advertised start and finish times? Are agendas published a set number of days in advance? Are minutes kept and circulated to those present in good time for the next meeting of that group?

Responding to clients

Do you have a policy for how teachers respond to queries, requests for information and other communication from parents? Within 24 hours? Three days? On headed paper? Typed or hand-written? If this is not important to you, then so be it. If it *is* important, then where is the quality standard and how would you know if there was a defect? What *should* matter to you is how the telephone is answered. This may seem a trivial issue but take it as axiomatic that outsiders, and especially other educationalists, make subjective, unreasonable and totally unfair assumptions about schools from the way in which the telephone is answered. You may not be a great fan of the 'Hi, I'm Bobbie, how may I help you and have-a-nice-day' school of telephone etiquette but at least find out whether the telephone is answered promptly and in a welcoming manner.

Meeting expectations

If you didn't like zero-defect or found it uncomfortable, then the notion a of a service meeting expectation or specification may be more helpful. If you have ever attended a seminar on quality you will be familiar with the example (for some reason it is always cars that are cited) of the Rolls-Royce and the Lada, or the Mercedes and the Mini. The example usually concerns a range of conceivable defects but the message is always the same: if you pay a lot or a little for a car you still want the car to meet an expectation aroused in your mind. If the cheap car therefore has low running costs, is reliable and retains its advertised resale value then that, for you, is a quality car. If the expensive car, however, has bits dropping off on day one then you will be irrationally distressed at your expectation of quality being dashed. That, for you, is no longer a quality car.

What expectations are you arousing with your clients in school? When appealing to potential parents through publicity material or in public meetings, school leaders are apt to be very expansive about what the youngsters can expect. The science area is always buzzing with fascinating technology and showy experiments, the library always has interesting and topical displays, and the school's star gymnasts are constantly engaged in Olympian feats. The teachers always have time for a lot of one-to-one attention for pupils. The curriculum promises a cornucopia of enrichment and extension beyond the mundanities of the legal requirements. This is all fair play and indeed parents who visit a lot of schools might be suspicious at the *absence* of these promises. More seriously, however, school leaders should be very careful about the detail of some of these expectations. It is sad but instructive to reflect on the experiences of that generation of parents in the UK whose children entered previously selective schools which had been reorganized as comprehensives. Whatever disclaimers schools made, and however much teachers pointed to the new realities, many of those parents assumed that their children were going to a 'better' kind of school and would therefore achieve what pupils in those 'better' schools achieved.

Where you are arousing practical expectations about access to sport and culture, about parental access to teachers and about range and choice within the curriculum, you must be doubly careful. Parents who have genuine complaints later on and who can remind you that you promised a particular level of service and response have a powerful case.

Quality control and quality assurance

The final aspect of the quality debate which is both worth taking on board and which has practical application is the difference between these two terms and the implications for school leaders of that difference. Briefly, the difference between 'quality control' and 'quality assurance' is like one of those eternal dualisms which seem to characterize human behaviour. To trust or to supervise? To control or to delegate? To expect individuals to have a sense of quality or to impose that quality through rule and procedure? Quality control implies checking at the process and at the output ends of the educational process. It implies sampling and inspecting and it assumes objective measures of quality. Quality assurance, on the other hand, implies that all the active partners in the transaction have a real sense of what counts as quality in terms of both their own contribution to the school's performance and what the school as a whole is trying to achieve. So much for definitions. There is something deeper involved here which goes to the heart of the school leader's approach to his or her job. It can be summarized by these questions;

- Do you trust teachers to do the best possible job with the minimum of supervision, interference or control?
- Do you believe that periodic checks, inspections and reporting make teachers do a better job?
- What are the circumstances of accountability which enable the best possible job to be done?

Such questions are tough to answer. You may want to say 'Yes, but...' or 'No, but...' to the first two and 'It depends' to the third. In your own situation as a school leader you may instinctively feel that quality assurance is exactly what most staff practice but that control is what a few need! Unfortunately, you have to do your best to build a climate in which *all* staff have similar expectations of their accountabilities. Although a modern rhetoric of collegiality and professionalism suggests that it is only through quality assurance (as opposed to quality control) that schools can deliver that best possible service, most leaders will find it hard to follow that approach completely. Agreeing quality standards, looking hard at zero-defect where applicable and being tough on meeting specifications are hard enough. Even in the most liberal climate of school leadership, the leader still needs to account, often personally, for the quality of what goes on. Where the results of that account are ambiguous or otherwise flawed, he or she must intervene. Such intervention, however dressed up and euphemized, is still about quality control.

Summary

Accountability is one of the essential dimensions of school leadership. Leaders do not operate in a vacuum. Teachers who are not leaders do not feel sensitive to the school's accountabilities in the same way that you do. Successful school leaders turn accountability into an active process: they take accountabilities as starting points rather than as end-points for their leadership. They want to demonstrate their school's successes rather than simply meet outside requirements for reporting and information. It is profoundly debilitating to see accountability as a necessary evil or an unwelcome intrusion on the smooth running of the school. It is immensely liberating to see accountability as an opportunity to pursue your vision of the future of your school.

References

Blake, R and Mouton, J (1985) *The Managerial Grid III*, Houston: Gulf.

Blanchard, K (1985) 'Situational leadership model', in Blanchard, K *et al*, (eds) *Leadership and the One-minute Manager*, London: Fontana/ Collins.

Burns, J M (1978) *Leadership*, New York: Harper & Row.

DePree, M (1989) *Leadership is an Art*, New York: Dell (Doubleday).

Etzioni, A (1964) *Modern Organizations*, New Jersey: Prentice Hall.

Fullan, M (1991) *The New Meaning of Educational Change*, Columbia University: Teachers' Press.

Herzberg, F, Mausner, B and Snyderman, B (1959) *The Motivation to Work*, New York: Harper & Row.

Hodgkinson, C (1978) *Towards a Philosophy of Administration*, Oxford: Blackwell.

Holmes, G and Neilson, A (1988) 'Headteachers or managers? Cultures in conflict?', *Journal of European Industrial Training*, **12**, 8.

Kanter, R M (1989) *When Giants Learn to Dance*, New York: Touchstone Press.

LEAP (1990) *Local Management in Schools*, Milton Keynes: Leap/BBC.

Maslow, A (1970) *Motivation and Personality*, New York: Harper & Row.

Peters, T and Waterman, R (1982) *In Search of Excellence*, London: Harper & Row.

Peters, T (1989) *Thriving on Chaos*, London: Pan.

Peters, T (1992) *Liberation Management – Necessary disorganization for the nano-second Nineties*, New York: A A Knopf.

Sergiovanni, T (1991) *Moral Leadership*, San Francisco, CA: Jossey-Bass.

Index